GW00726141

Richard Kell was born in Co. Cork in 1927. After spending five years in India he was educated in Ireland. In 1983 he retired from his post as a senior lecturer in English Literature to devote more time to creative work. He has produced five individual volumes of poetry: *Control Tower* (1962), *Differences* (1969), *The Broken Circle* (1981), *In Praise of Warmth: New & Selected Poems* (1987) and *Rock and Water* (1993). Between 1960 and 1973 he was a poetry reviewer for *The Guardian* and *The Critical Survey*. He has published articles and short stories in magazines, has written a number of essays, and for approximately 47 years kept a reflective journal, now in typescript and entitled *The Banyan Book*.

COLLECTED POEMS 1962-1993

COLLECTED POEMS 1962-1993

RICHARD KELL

LAGAN PRESS
BELFAST
2001

Published by
Lagan Press
138 University Avenue
Belfast BT7 1GZ

© Richard Kell 2001

© Introduction, Fred Johnston, 2001

The moral right of the author has been asserted.

ISBN: 1 873687 12 5

Author: Kell, Richard
Title: Collected Poems 1962-1993
2001

Cover Design: December
Set in New Baskerville
Printed by Noel Murphy Printing, Belfast

to the memory of Muriel (1924-75) & Colin (1955-95)
and for Carolyn, Timothy and Shelagh

CONTENTS

UNCOLLECTED POEMS

Preface

When poetry is published, what matters most is the reader's experience; but since another person's experiences have coloured the poetry, a few biographical details may make it more easily approachable. Hence the main content of this preface. The shortest entry in *The Banyan Book,* a reflective journal I kept for about 47 years, is 'My work, not me'. I still feel that poems, as well as many kinds of ideas, are given—that they come from some part of our minds which won't be coerced or coaxed. Of course this refers to the opening drafts of poems, formal or not; the technique that goes mainly into revision is applied deliberately. But even then a phrase that seems just right may appear from nowhere. My earliest poem, written when I was nine, included the words 'a song that none may find'. Though they referred to birdsong, did they reveal a child's sense of creative mystery?

I'd like to quote now the whole of the first stanza, which is all I remember:

Little robin redbreast sits upon a tree,
Singing to you and singing to me,
Singing a song that none may find,
Comforting the lame ones and comforting the blind.

Sits? If the rest of the poem suffered from similar ineptitudes, maybe its fall into oblivion was no bad thing. But the sentiments of that stanza, though a bit inept in other ways, can be seen as an indirect tribute to my various upbringers. I value also the proverbs handed down to me—probably dismissed by some people nowadays as expressions of petit-bourgeois prudence: 'You're not the only pebble on the beach', 'It's no use crying over spilt milk', 'Look before you leap', 'A stitch in time saves nine', 'Do the work that's nearest/Though it's dull at whiles,/Helping, when you meet them,/Lame dogs over stiles'. I don't suppose you've met any more lame dogs at stiles than I have, but the underlying thought is praiseworthy. As an incorrigible universalist I like to believe that such thoughts, far from being merely local and bourgeois, are a part of the world's folk wisdom, and that they have arisen from a need to be firm and resourceful in the face of many threatening realities.

My present tribute is to my father George and his relatives, from the North of Ireland, and to my mother Irene and hers, from the South. In both cases the immediate roots were Protestant and 'British'. I say immediate because, if we go back far enough, we'll all find ourselves extremely mixed. Apart from the fact that mixtures have been around since the year dot, I'm entirely in favour of them. (That's what the universe is like: unity with diversity—not uniformity, which is what the bullies would like to impose.)

My father was at first a teacher and then a Methodist clergyman. My elder brother Donald and I were born during his ministry in Youghal, Co. Cork. We then travelled with him and our mother to the mission field in South India, where our siblings Mary and Alan were born. The Nilgiri Hills provided the wonderful green environs of our bungalow near Ketti, and of Hebron High School, which Donald and I attended as boarders.

Later we started as boarders at Methodist College Belfast ('Methody') while our parents, accompanied by Mary and Alan, returned to India. The Cork grandparents then became our guardians and we had delightful holidays to look forward to. I remember William Musgrave and May (née Evans) with deep affection. Willie, as everyone called him, was the manager of the Metropole Hotel and a notable personality. Being in Belfast when he died, Donald and I were spared attendance at his funeral, but I was pleased to hear later that the cortège, as well as being unusually long, included many Catholics. I have warm memories also of May's sister Ada, who had remained single and was the Metropole's manageress. In her famous Room 96 she often entertained the two of us with sandwiches and absorbing readings. The room overlooked Musgrave Brothers' sweet factory, from which delicious smells arose.

With our paternal grandparents, Alexander and Catherine(née Arnold), we spent many pleasurable weekends in

Finaghy, a suburb of Belfast. 'Grandpa Kell' had been a mill foreman and a flute player in the mill's band, and was still a Methodist lay preacher. I must mention also my father's sister Evie and her chemist husband Roy Ballentine, who were equally endearing weekend hosts in Lisburn and later in Lurgan. After seven years at Methody I was educated in Dublin, first at Wesley College and then at university (TCD). While I was still at Wesley I wrote a short descriptive poem called 'Pigeons', which was to be included in many anthologies, in radio programmes, and even in an exam paper and a verse-speaking competition. Meanwhile, hiding behind the astonishing pseudonym Harold Grove, I sent it off to Bruce Williamson of the *Irish Times*. It appeared—my first publication outside school magazines—on the literary page in 1946, the year it was written.

During the undergraduate years I enjoyed the friendly and helpful interest of Robert Greacen, Sam Harrison, Billy O'Sullivan and Ben Howard—all older than me—and of Pearse Hutchinson, the same age as myself. Among my undergraduate friends were Geoff Wilde, Stewart Cross, and Bill Webb, who was to become the literary editor of *The Guardian*. With them I shared a keen interest in composing and performing music. Others I was closely associated with, partly in editing the magazine *Icarus*, were Alec Reid, Bernard Share and—now well-known as the creator of Inspector Ghote—Harry Keating. These and many others I remember with admiration and affection.

While living as a student in digs I began to keep the journal mentioned above. I filled several early pages with smart thoughts about the effects of a religious upbringing; but shortly afterwards I cut them out, judging them self-centred, ungenerous, and much too speculative. Though I have since then moved far from my parents and grandparents in spiritual matters, I see that their concerns and mine have had the same origin, and am grateful for their loving seriousness. Certain New Testament ideas, combined with Romantic ones, pointed the way to spiritual humanism and the Western mystical tradition, and these to Hinduism, Buddhism and Taoism. Later I saw possible links between such philosophies (collectively the Perennial Philosophy) and post-Newtonian science—as did some of the founders and subsequent exponents of quantum theory. These interests appear in a number of poems.

After graduation I wanted only to go on writing verse, prose, and music. Relatives and friends with a stronger sense of reality suggested that a diploma in education might be useful: it would at least be 'something to fall back on'. Reluctantly I took their advice and, armed with the necessary qualification, spent a term teaching English and French at Kilkenny College. I can't remember why I then decided to accept a post at a Middlesbrough school. This was one of the very few schools, whether Irish or English, to have responded to my many applications—the others, perhaps, having shrewdly detected what was lurking between the lines. Still, I made an effort through the years and was finally appointed to teach degree students at Newcastle-upon-Tyne Polytechnic, now the University of Northumbria. From that 13-year post I took early retirement in 1983.

Muriel Nairn, born and bred in Dublin, had done me the honour of becoming my wife thirty years previously. We had four fine children: Colin, Carolyn, Timothy, and Shelagh. This rich and complex period of my life cannot be dealt with in a preface, but several poems try to tell a small part of the story that included Muriel's death in 1975. Twenty years after that sad event we were to lose Colin as well.

There's another story too—about a widower's experiences with a few successive partners. Again there are poems that suggest a certain amount as best they can. Let me just add to the family history a note of heartfelt thanks to each of the companions who, in spite of many difficulties, generously shared some years of my post-marital life.

Most ageing authors are probably curious to know how much they've written. I recently discovered that from 1946 to 1992—the first and last years of *composition* represented in this book—I produced (or was given) about 650 poems, not counting one with 4000 lines. Many of those—among them a handful written for fun, as presents, or just as a way of letting off steam—were never submitted to magazines. But quantity of output is unimportant: what may interest a few readers is the proportion of that total offered in the following pages. It is a little under forty per cent—including the poems in the final section, most of them published but none previously collected. Some readers might prefer an even lower figure; but here, for better or worse, are the choices of one writer and, from 1946 to 1992, quite a few editors.

I would like to express my gratitude to all at the Lagan Press, to those who published my work in earlier years (including magazine editors), and to the friends and relatives who have shown an encouraging interest.

My warm thanks also to Fred Johnston for taking on the heroic task of writing a critical introduction.

Richard Kell
August 2000

Introduction

In terms of poetry, we live in a silly age. Poets rush to publish, often from their own presses, collected or selected editions of their work, assuming rather audaciously that there is a public anxiously awaiting them. Usually, there isn't, the whole thing merely another exercise in egotism.

When a poet collects the product of years of writing and sifts for those poems he would wish to get, as it were, a second hearing, he is examining sections of his own life. There is a considerable responsibility involved. It is much more than a business of literary editing. A collected edition of a poet's work is also a portal through which a public, hopefully a new one, can peer at the creative life and judge the work anew. It is no light undertaking.

The poetry of Richard Kell might properly be lined up, as he hints in his Preface, with contemporaries such as Sam Harrison and Robert Greacen, both of whom he knew at Trinity College, Dublin. These poets emerged in an age when poetry meant something quite different from what it means today. Poetry was not, then, another form of show-business; had not, in the words of poet and editor William Oxley, "become so emptied of precise meaning in our time." For young poets, Eliot, Auden, MacNeice too, hovered over much of the poetry being written; and there was the sadder yet equally potent shadow of poets who had written through a second world war, some not surviving it. Poetry and the age were intertwined. Equally, the heroic, almost crusading, idealism of the Spanish Civil War impressed poets too young to have participated in it.

Richard Kell's published poetry began at the end of World War II.

Represented here are five books (there are fifty other poems which have not seen book-form), a very humane poetry of involvement and concern, personal or otherwise.

To our shame, Kell is now, in my view, a critically neglected poet. This, in spite of his having been a respected poetry reviewer for *The Guardian*. There is a wide variety of reasons for a poet not being given the attention he deserves. One of them is change of style; there are also market forces at work. Poets who brought a required elegance and honed stylistic force to their work are overlooked all too often in favour of those who lack both but are more presentable in the gaudy theatre poetry has become.

But Kell's work is always modern, contemporary, immediate. From the earliest work represented here, *Control Tower* (1962), bleak, crafted irony is coupled with a meticulous sense of rhythm:

> Over the injured ground
> where pick and shovel probed—
> cutting away the soil
> like flesh around the drain—

> — 'Watchman'

Curiously, the poem bears the authority of a war-poem, although it isn't one. This could be a poem of the London blitz. The bleak 'Sidings,' however, is a very different poem, narrative, lightly MacNeicean, speculative, using flexible rhyming lines:

> Sunlight and silence. Yet not unaware
> when fists of smoke pummel the distant air
> and the long locomotives thunder past,
> clattering over points: a seismic blast
> shudders across the network; ...

The simple dramatic power of 'the long locomotives thunder past' is a line younger, brasher poets might learn from. The long poem itself shunts into philosophical speculation; towns are 'trite/unlovely', commerce is 'inane,' 'nervous boredom' the reaction. Britain still had its bombed acres, its bombed-in memories; towns and cities rebuilt themselves, well into the 50s. There was, arguably, a reaction of sensitivity against the urban life, its implied tedium, its dead-stop certainties. The psyche longed for more than a promise of routine.

But for Kell, the rural too offers little salvation. 'The Woods' is a frightening, ominous poem, the described natural world, however yearned for, remains a place where innocence dies. A poem to Kierkegaard and poems such as 'Kwan Yin Gives Her Explanation' and 'Firmament' indicate the thinking of a poet whose religious upbringing not surprisingly was paving the way for a variety of spiritual meditations.

Differences (1969) is somewhat more audacious. 'Dreams' is a dark sequence, eight titled poems in all; in 'The City' a Blakean vision is offered, where "windows spilt/unearthly light, and in my heart made/such happiness that I cried." (Interesting, the motif of a train in 'The Woman', appearing out of nowhere into a scene reminiscent of speculations in James Frazer's *The Golden Bough*. This heady mix of pseudo-myth and actuality was not unknown to poets such as Robert Graves and arguably constitutes another symptom of a poeticised revolt against urban modernism; in Graves' case, a frankly post war reaction). 'Dreams' is an odd sequence, bearing one down to the drear of offices and up into visionary bursts of light. It is, in another sense, a very modern and a very personal one; an epiphany is hinted at. In a city, the mythic is possible. Urban epiphanies are necessary if the urban is to be tolerated: 'Plain Human' is a darkly hopeful poem in which a sense of self-acceptance (urbanised, routined) is reached only after painful progress through realisation of a spirituality—never an exact word—which cannot in any case properly be achieved:

Day after day I ask myself
precisely what

this worry-go-round is meant for;
and sometimes I look out
at the garden, which is a wilderness,
and I am caught

in a small calm of seeing: ...

'The Veteran' and the harrowing 'Dolores' are seemingly emblematic of a shadow presiding over this period of Kell's poetry; images of preservation, of blind survival, scar the landscape of this selection.

New things happen by the time of *The Broken Circle* (1981). 'Sky Poem' carries us into rarefied yet rejuvenating air and even if "the flier, for all his art, can only droop/to a field in the middle of nowhere," we are out of the way of heaving trains, billboards, and survivors. The 'airiness' of this poem and the neat rhythm of a second-fourth line rhyme in the quatrains is like fresh air and we are invited to sail in it. Freed of something, the poems travel, to Africa, to Ulster, in and out of religious ceremony, interesting, informative, a poet seeing the wonder in ordinary things without the impediment of wondrous visions. As Kell tells us in 'Skills,'

... I love watching the bricks fall ...

The result is clearer sight to a real, vibrant world. There are poems here of reflection on childhood. 'Walking with Matron' is a marvellous, darkly humorous poem, describing an Eden in which this particular Eve batters the threatening reptile to death:

... But near the school we halted,
while Matron lifted her walking-stick and battered
a small brown snake to death, her spectacles glowing.

It is part of the 'grand scale' nature of Kell's poetry to embrace the sudden natural treachery of life, in a poem such as 'Lofthouse Colliery, 1973,' for instance (" ... he gave/his lonely mind to whatever it meant to die/buried already in a violent grave.") and write so movingly of love. 'Heartwood' is a sequence of poems to Kell's late wife, Muriel; but it is prefaced, if you like, by the lyrical and fond 'Spring Night,' a 1952 poem with a soothsaying ominous music to it:

... I could not tell you
I was afraid of something out there
in the future, like that dark and bitter sea: ...

In Praise of Warmth: New & Selected Poems, came out in 1987. By now much of Kell's work has established its pattern; there is a quizzical, interrogative broodiness, a concern for life married uneasily with a refusal to be deceived by appearances, to sentimentalise nature—for all that early suspicion of the urban—

and a distinct, Audenesque lyricism informing, occasionally, important love poems. Kell has been painting his age, an age of discernible spiritual and social confusions; ironically, by the Eighties, love poems were suspect in the new culture, yet Kell wrote them anyway and kept the faith:

I search for the smallest clue—
no longer to find out
what suffering is all about,
but filled with the memory of you—
— 'A Faith in Music'

With a nod in the direction of the Elizabethans, Kell conjures up 'Death's Reply,' a sombre, disciplined poem out of its time, one might argue, but an attack upon it, a refusal of it, too:

I am not proud, nor do I seek dominion;
I do not destroy, or even sting.
Fire stings, and the nettle, and the scorpion;
violence breeds in every natural thing.

Kell's general view of life, expressed in earlier poems, is highlighted here; the natural world cannot be trusted, even though he views its destruction with regret. He was writing this at a time when younger poets were going head-to-head with the world, tossing aside the lyric, ignoring the great poetic themes, often creating a non-poetry in the process. 'Realism' was leading to a rejection of poetry as something that illuminated the human condition. Kell, however, was not unaware of the change. Some things, perhaps, could never be said again, at least not in the same way. 'To The Skylark Again' contains the telling lines:

If only you knew,
remote in your urban pastoral,
how celebrated you are —
'blithe spirit,' 'pilgrim of the sky,'
soul of a violin rhapsody
ascending from a green shire.
That flight is over now except
in the Eng Lit syllabus ...

The poem goes on to suggest that urban roar drowns what dream the lark, or anything of the natural world, can offer, while at the same time upholding the virtues at the heart of romantic poetry.

Many of Kell's poems struggle with the contradictions imposed by the desire for a less complex world and the need to, in some sense, accommodate it and reveal it. One might speculate whether these contrarieties may even be the result of his Southern-Northern parentage. In fact much of Kell's poetry is informed by the nature of contradictions; the able, perhaps romantic, lyricist vies with the pessimist whose world-view is in turn informed by an almost tangible melancholy. It might be argued that such conditions applied to any poet who, adolescent in the last world war, matured in a Britain where the sober Fifties gave way to the supposedly 'Swinging' Sixties; only to retrench again in the money-cultured Thatcherite years. I believe it is impossible to divorce the formation of Kell's poetry from the formation of his times and this is one quality which makes him immensely readable. He can be forgiven his pessimism.

Rock and Water visits the 90s. The maturity of these poems, the confident stride of their language and form, permits the poet to use denser, more narrative structures and reveal their investigative possibilities. At the same time, a short poem, 'This Be The Converse' is a gentle repudiation of Larkin's famous poem, and, presumably, Larkin's own pessimism:

> They buck you up, your mum and dad,
> or if they don't they clearly should ...

He goes on to fling a sharp aside at contemporary culture and its inarticulateness, its pride in un-learning and its rooted shallowness:

> y've had some big hits so y're where it's at
> bein an artist makin the reviewers
> rave n havin yr talent reckonised
> I mean like y've arrived ...
>
> — 'Star Quality'

This Burgess-speak inability to communicate intelligently — or the renovation of poetic language, for example, the dumbing-down of poetry ,in another context—is one of the by-products of a society broken on the rack of crazed cultural liberalism and notions that everyone is an artist no matter how incoherent and unintelligible. Politics certainly is untrustworthy—at the very least the terminology, the language of it is—and mock-socialism and the paradoxical desire to be 'upper class' in accent if nothing else (this is all very relevant, particularly in the Republic of Ireland, one might add) makes ideological traitors of us all:

... preserve us from, but let us still enjoy,
leftwing equivalents of Bertie Wooster.
                    — 'After Bumping into X Yet Again'

The last section of poems, uncollected and starting in 1947, offers a reflective grandeur moving towards a sure stylistic voice. Again, the concerns range from the speculative, to notions of grief, to the business of creating art. Kell's gift is to bring us down gently — at least some of the time — from the airless heights of illusion to the earthier confines of self-realisation, a not unpainful process. The urban is magical, or comprehensible ('Night in the City,' 'City Spring'), if we can but stop to look; salvation is a personal thing, however, and one fashions it how one will:

That you feel pain and doubt
thinking beyond such things,
troubled by a phantom's
insidious whisperings,
or by a private grief
that drags you from the vision,
this is what makes you grope
for some precise illusion
concocting faith from hope.
                    — 'That You Feel Joy and Peace.'

Towards the end, however, and curiously, the second world war sneaks in by the back door, allowing comparisons with Ulster's troubles:

The sirens, weird and sickening, made a smear
of harmony on the air, wormed back to hell,
and left a silence like projected fear,
a tranced alertness while the clouds were frisked
by searchlights ...

...

... Through years of failure, while the spirit drains
out of a province, furtive bigots creep
in their own murk with gelignite and gun,
hoping that their guerrilla talk will blur
the hard black outline of the murderer.

— 'Bombers'

The word 'smear' in the first line is horrifyingly ugly and
blood-filled; 'wormed back to hell' has a harrowing Elizabethan
black feel to it. Kell's use of the word 'guerrilla' may serve to
remind us that, arguably, the word 'gurrier' has a similar root.
Kell is careful with his use of language, however poised and
stylish it may appear to be; he does not over-write and his voice is
always sensible. Nowadays it is not done for critics to suggest that
poems are beautiful; meaningful is considered a far more
important word. This is a nonsense; some of Kell's poems are
indeed beautiful by any aesthetic standard and they are sincerely
meaningful into the bargain. It may be too much to suggest that
Kell is, in varying ways, a 'war' poet, but there is evidence to
suggest that war and civic violence (poverty, social deprivation,
the dehumanising effect of some forms of progress) have been
dealt with in more than a few of his serious poems and have
prompted in others—even, perhaps, some of the gentler poems
—a noticeable pessimism. In a savage little poem,
'Opportunism,' based on a Reith Lecture, there appear the
cutting lines:

That the war may be continued
That there may be expenditure on weapons
That industry may flourish ...

Kell is very much a poet of his time and ours in that he

reminds us that societal progress is dominated by factors often too ugly to contemplate, such as war, famine and greed.

From the end of the second world war to the cultural laying-waste of Thatcherism, the creation of a New World Order and disturbing poems on the war against Iraq, is hardly an upwards progress in many respects. Kell suggests this, while attempting to resolve conflicts of cultural and socio-political imperative in himself. Moreover, he is acutely aware in his work that we live in a faithless age; much of what is served up as contemporary visual or literary art bears this out.

Always it is the personal, the intensely small, the everyday disillusion of the unwritten individual which creates recognisable history. Richard Kell's own griefs percolate into ours and the larger ones of a society lacking faith in anything outside itself. Not to read him is to remain blind to the fact of there having been recorders of this small and great history from the end of a world war—his first truly published poem appearing in the *Irish Times* in 1946—to the street-to-street destructions of a provincial one, that these writers were British-Irish and consequently lived in some sort of unconscious exile, and that their birthland has been disregarding of their commentary, their soundness of judgement and, above all, their crafted, meticulous, poetic ability. Richard Kell, let it be said, is a very good poet.

Theirs was not necessarily a more elegant age—in many obvious respects it was more terrible—but it was arguably more cultured, more lettered and conscious of the redeeming power of poetry and literature. And notions of belief, such as patriotism, doing the right thing, honour maligned, threadbare concepts in our New Ireland, certainly—still counted for something.

The best poems of Kell and others of his generation speak warningly to us at a time when our exile from poetry into a lost land of the trite and trivial is almost complete; the point, as Pound says in another context, 'when separation had come to its worst.' Perhaps, as for the exiles in Pound's poem, a meeting between redemption and poetry is at hand at just such a crucial point. Perhaps too, poetry such as that of Richard Kell can encourage us to boot the moneychangers out of our cultural temples.

Fred Johnston
September 2000

CONTROL TOWER
(1962)

CHARIOTS

Day was unkind to these,
emphasising the sullen grime-etched face,
the droop of blinkered heads, the imperative bit,
imposing a heavy load and a tortoise pace.

Dusk flicks a generous wand:
like a reminiscence the empty coal carts spill
from the dimness as though from entombed antiquity,
to claim their lordly moment down the hill.

Four in a daredevil race
pass dark shuttles of rhythm through twilight's loom.
These swaying taut silhouettes are bodies that sagged;
indifference now has burst to a sudden bloom

of zest. Sleek necks outstretched—
a rhyme of limbs where an ancient instinct moves,
waking a ghost of thunder from dead arenas—
the horses spatter jewels from stabbing hooves.

FISHING HARBOUR TOWARDS EVENING

Slashed clouds leak gold. Along the slurping wharf
the snugged boats creak and seesaw. Round the masts

abrasive squalls flake seagulls off the sky:
choppy with wings the rapids of shrill sound.

Wrapt in spliced airs of fish and tar,
light wincing on their knives, clockwork men

incise and scoop the oily pouches, flip
the soft guts overboard with blood-wet fingers.

Among three rhythms the slapping silver turns
to polished icy marble upon the deck.

WATCHMAN

Over the injured ground
    where pick and shovel probed—
cutting away the soil
    like flesh around the drain—
over the jagged stones
    red lanterns pin the dark,
and brazier light forgets
    the solar glare of pain.

Loneliness, like the wind,
    sneaks in: the watchman's mind
grows draughty now. Across
    the brooding serious eyes
a twist of smoke uncurls:
    gently the pipe-dreams rise,
the immaculate suave hotels,
    the music, the slim girls.

His thoughts lie low, fearing
    the infinite sky, the trees
exposed like nerves to the wind's
    abrasion, starlight spilling
down the long approach
    of love, to love's darkness,
that wears the lantern rubies
    like a brooch.

SWANS AT NIGHT

Into the brief reality
of pallid lamps and grinning
neon surveillance of the plunge
to pleasure, they are swimming,
adagio of flutes
over a heady counterpoint.
With the magic of a myth,
quietly past the blunt
knees of the bridge, rumpling
a redsilk circle of water,
they come from dream, coldly
consummate into a smatter
of warm half-living: as though
forms of another reality
to which we are strangers here
in the plangent city.

ADOLESCENCE

A slinky fur of rain invites those lovers,
but hurts the young man wandering alone,
whose fear and shame, bred of misinformation,
curl like a tapeworm in the active will.

He has yawned away the routine hours,
waiting for dusk to slide a copper sun
into the night's juke-box, and travels now
the slick seductive pavements of his lust.

Friendly, concerned, the movie screen applies
an unguent music when the censor jabs.
Midnight he prowls his greenhorn wilderness,
watching the lamplit whores he dare not touch.

Locked power disturbs him where the sour canal
delineates his mood. (Those swans deceive
none who observed the yellow scum, the tins
rusting among the weeds, the dead dogs floating.)

A pit of darkness gouged beneath the sluice
receives the trickling pus of dammed-up water,
night after night recalling what befell
the swiftness and the clarity of love.

THE HOLIDAY MAKERS

Along the pier on lazy summer evenings
    they wander into leisure.
For this the day was made; they shall not feel—
    haunting their easy pleasure
in talk of little things—the smouldering fear
    that broods like threat of thunder
above the still horizon of tomorrow,
    for they have rested under
the gentle laws that sanction and renew
    their talk of little things,
like gulls their laughter light enough to move
    with slender glassy rings
only the polished surfaces of selves.

    Cool in their eyes
the sea's flickering blue, the poised yachts.

The curving sails surprise
a love whose gifted sight their lives have dazed.
    (Something here of scrolled
petals that startle you from self-concern;
    something of minds that hold
desire away from the furnace of the heart
    like wind precise and cold
fashioned to these smooth contours.) This way too
    they watch the mailboat swing
beyond the pier, spading the water back,
    and lift their hands and fling
goodbye, half gay, half sad, across the evening
    to friends they never met
but know exactly in the ritual moment.

    This gesture will forget
how they betray the love that time recaptures,
    when neither carefree words
nor petals nor a moulded wind can please them,
    and those white birds
are folded in their grooves of rock. The selves
    they shaped with careful skill,
artists of leisure on a summer evening,
    elude the finest will.
The lonely yachts lie stripped like winter trees;
    against the landing stage
the empty mailboat stands aloof and silent.
    And beauty turns to rage
meeting those friends, who were eternal strangers.

INNOCENCE

As children they would not compromise,
they spent their love and hate with swift conviction;
    their glances told no lies.

For such pure egoists the name
was quite irrelevant till some wistful tutor
    carefully taught them shame.

And then it made some sense, for they
discovered rival claims and clipped their passions
    and were no longer gay.

Where once with innocence they could turn
all things to their advantage, now they're thought
    guilty of self-concern.

In small talk you will see their eyes
flicker and fight, searching for love again
    and trying to tell lies.

SIDINGS

You'd hardly believe that half-forgotten track
had anything to do with crack express
or labouring goods train. It does not end,
but pauses there: the colon buffers lend
an interim finality, as though
fifty yards more or less were no
matter for argument. Simply to be
right there is pleasant—an inlet where the sea
of industry and trade quietly laps
on grass and nettles, a flower or two; perhaps
a sparrow dances on the polished metals.

Sunlight and silence. Yet not unaware
when fists of smoke pummel the distant air
and the long locomotives thunder past,
clattering over points: a seismic blast
shudders across the network; the siding quivers.
But happy now with the music of a squat
tank engine shunting in the hot
and peaceful forenoon, clinking lines of trucks.

Those trains, those people. Travelling endlessly
the tedious circuits of economy.
It knows itself included (rightly so,
owing its contribution). But they go
too far, it thinks; they go too fast, and lose
their souls in making money, making news.
Simply to be right here, alone, to make
a dream for wholeness' sake—
from sunlight, polished rails, a flower or two,
is better in the long run.

                              Whistles blew;
the noise of luggage barrows, jets of steam
slashing suddenly against the grain

of reverie, clipped my thoughts into the plain
square box of commonsense, which knows
that sidings presuppose
something to be aside from. Do away
with that (so all can dream), and then you may
destroy the gift of dreaming and create
a wilderness of tracks that merely wait—
with no through-lines to make them meaningful—
watching the little engines push and pull
backwards and forwards aimlessly all day,
until the clinking music that they play
sickens the ear with boredom. If you'd save
those dreams, you must restore the plan that gave
the shunting relevance; and if you'd claim
some value for your dreaming, scorn the tame
refusal of the sidings, which invoke
the privilege of being where the stroke
of pistons and the metre of the wheels
are leisurely and mild, or distance feels
the impassioned emphasis of speed
a drowsy evocation, not a need.
Allow no anodyne for discontent,
but give the mind a structure taut and fine,
guarding that clarity, that stillness where
all valid dreams begin.
                              I paid my fare,
boarded the train, secured a window seat
and sank into a wave of dust and heat;
then, carried into sunshine, watched the trite
unlovely town withdrawing out of sight,
terrace by dismal terrace, lane by lane,
mile after mile reciting the inane
tautology of commerce.

                              I recalled
those two soliloquies, and found the moral
suspect either way. For there's no quarrel
native here: no *ought*, but *is*, provides
the self that is not changed by changing sides.
Those were the facts—those hoardings, walls, backyards—
a nervous boredom my response. What guards
what clarity and stillness for what dream?
Merely an attitude, that may redeem
a sullen mood, but is as changeable
as moods themselves, answering to the pull
of any clever argument it needs.
And what reflective programme that secedes
from high-powered competition saves a soul?

(To be right there is pleasant, not a dole
for moral indigence.)

The beat of metal
on metal speeded up and the metre broke
splintering over points. The punching smoke
fattened and fluffed, then hovered down the line,
thinning out to a drowsy evocation.
And never reached its proper destination,
the peaceful and idyllic, where a clink
of trucks defined the stillness ... Better think
of something else. So much of me was there,
I must forget, or travel to despair.

KIERKEGAARD
Without the risk, faith is an impossibility.

I have three plans to choose from on this island,
and every one a risk. Should I sail forth
with scant provisions in a tiny boat,
and set my course toward the crystal north,
drowned or starved the loss I bear is double.
And so it is if I should seek the south,
plodding through jungle, swamp and treacherous desert,
no wand of water touch my withered mouth,
and vultures pick the autumn from my bones.
If neither sea nor sand should make my grave,
but lazy I watch this palm tree dust the moon,
I tempt the fury of the tidal wave.

But no, he says; though three alternatives,
you have a single choice: to put to sea
and aim your bows toward the grim horizon,
while love is softly washing on the lee.
There is no time to rummage in reflection
or lust and lounge with animal aplomb.
(The big green book lies open on my hand
and ticks away the seconds like a bomb.)

IN THE BEGINNING

God was the first poem ever uttered
by innocent astonished lips, when doubt
had dropped a pebble in the water's trance,
the image of Narcissus cracked and rippled.
Then nothing was itself: always the hunters
prowled through metaphor, felt it underfoot
or brushing across their shoulders; saw it burst
above the jungle, slash the trees with rain,
dispensing love and anger like a giant.

And every poem was a souvenir
of the unending trek toward perfection
(lying surely beyond the steaming ridges,
the poisoned tracts of swamp). The eyes that once
like emeralds caught the light of simple beauty
were shaded now with terror, and the young
smooth stems of thought crumpled and cut like thorn-trees.
And all day long among the voiceless flowers,
the sunlight's tilted pillars, parrots gossiped,
and screeched with laughter at the goggling idols.

THE BURNING CRATE

Filled for the last time
the crate becomes a tank
of liquid crackling gold,
and gives the thirsty mind
refreshing light to drink.
Whose truth I would distil,
yet all the words are cold:
saying, earth's energies
declare a holy will.

Suppose I walk away,
wrench back when a sudden cry
falls round me like a noose,
and see the taloned fire
snatching a child at play:
should this renew the spell
(all opposites reconciled)
or instantly betray
a flaw, a casual hell
that mocks the power of choice

in man or simple child;
invoke my hands, my voice,
against the power that filled
the dark with life, and yet
as willingly destroys?

Though to love's urgency
I give my faith, being human,
the cold words haunt me still,
teaching us to admire
perfections that could kill
by accident in Eden;
and, from another myth
correcting our despair,
to fuse the dying with
the pity and the fire.

A SUPPLICANT SPEAKS OF THE GODDESS KWAN YIN

She was a human thought, a dainty protest
against the claims of godhead. We who loved life
and would have looked for truth in songs and flowers,
in wine and precious stones and women's beauty,
we could not take the Master at his word,
close up the shutters while the sun was climbing
and light the lamp indoors. The wise men gave us paradox;
some, being frightened by their cleverness,
locked themselves in for ever and stuffed the windows;
and some allowed themselves a compromise:
cherished the scents and colours in the garden,
yet were penitent when they threw a glance
at the slim girls walking in the street.
But we, uncertain of the ways of God,
too passionate or weak to crush desire,
or else too much afraid of death (supposing
the wise men were deluded),
we took the risk of sin and prayed for mercy.

Here is the goddess, head graciously tilted,
gentle and grave and wise, serenely smiling:
so we had come to think of her—a symbol
of pure mercy. But sometimes I have seen
a little harlot demure and yet coquettish,
her slender body made for men's hands,
and in the beauty of her brow and eyelids,

the pouting lips, the finger at her breast,
a hint of roguish humour and contempt.
It was as though we knew, in spite of all
our glossy thoughts, the Master's way was best;
as though our souls betrayed us into truth,
giving us back our dreams in this carved girl
with the sly face and small ambiguous hand.

KWAN YIN GIVES HER EXPLANATION

Sly and satirical you made me
as well as gentle and serene,
harlot confused with blessed lady
because the inner mind had seen
the truth you were evading.

Not that the Master's way is right,
but that you are fool and coward—
to have your sensual delight
and still avoid some moral hazard,
praying when you take fright.

Kill the self-pity you named Kwan Yin,
then call me lover instead of whore
and joyfully reinterpret sin.
Or smash my image, dance no more
and light the lamp within.

FIRMAMENT

Do not perturb the stillness of their faith,
whirlpool of fire renew, spitting stars,
that long ago their sorrow clenched and pruned
into a ball of gold. Manoeuvre this
bright globe that you have made, though twice as powerful,
at tranquil distances from all the rest;
or try a clash with one that's yet unrolled,
still waving enthusiastic arms of light.

Had you come nearer truth it would be something:
but what have they revealed, these white explosions,
this blazing dialectic? You began

adrift in space, and now, for all you've said,
you drift in space. And still that cold black sea
awards no certain glimpse of land ahead.

THE QUARREL AND THE JESTER

Hardly as tall
even as the kitchen table.
A pint-sized chucklehead
with a language of three words,
a blithe, believing eye,
a six-inch stride.

Something is going on
that's over his head. He trots
from knee to knee, drawing
out of the unsuspected
cold of the upper world
familiar warmth.

And like the fool
(without the fool's cunning)
keeps out of politics:
when rival courtiers glare
turns the indifferent glass
to any face,

recalling there
the quaint humanity.
In his bright underworld
something is going on:
he brings from fool to fool
their common love.

A WORD FOR MY SON

1

Look, the first reel
run off in memory, all
the bad bits cut away:
discoveries, thrills—the feel
of ice cream on your tongue,
the hop of a red ball.

Half-hours of trains that sprout
from sleepy distances,
bore through the wind, expand,
smash your taut trance, a clout
of steam-and-metal thunder
that crumbles, sifts, dies.

Barges down the canal,
dock leaves on glossy folds
of water launched and lilted,
the sunned air magical;
by dandelion clocks
the timeless hours told.

You at the airport, spellbound.
Tension of noise and speed,
slipstream playing the ground
glissando: floated clear
on the smooth modulation
the sun-slicked wings recede.

Richmond, Windsor, Kew:
long days of crowds and steamers,
picnics and daffodils.
Your eyes alive with new
puzzlements and convictions,
your sleeping rich with dreams.

2

The deadlife now: the flint.
Rare things are filed away
marked *Useless—Treat With Care,*
the seemly trash we stint
and hate for reinstated.
A man has bills to pay.

A child has things to learn
other than joy. (Not I,
not any human being,
authorised this.) The turn
of time leaves stinking pools
where poisons multiply.

You four, I thirty-two:
I know but do not feel
the way you feel. That knowledge
is my best gift to you
when love is mean, and pity
a construct of the will.

Yours is the same person
that prowled my ruined hours,
fretting in shadows, dodging
the white floodbeam of reason.
By the same twist you change
and brood, contentment sours.

Watching you sulk and whine,
your sense of wonder blurred,
where shall I seek—knowing
the demon also mine
and you too young for knowledge—
the purifying word?

THE BALANCE

Always the one that will not let me be—
when I would overflow (the mind free,
the heart ready to love, the voice to sing),
reminds me with its prudent nagging tongue

that life is such and such: the free mind,
the loving heart and singing voice are kind;
so plan, cherish, be provident, pay the bills:

the horses lumber, but the tiger kills.

Always the one that will not let me change—
when I'd be careful, sympathise, arrange
(the voice level, the mind about to freeze),
recalls what goodness tamed no longer sees,

that life is such and such: the frozen mind
and level voice are to themselves unkind;
then play, be prodigal, give joy its head:

the fountain's reckless, but the cistern's dead.

ENCOUNTER IN A READING ROOM

Good luck has entered, silky and black, padding
slowly towards the desk where I sit reading.
And idly superstitious I think, 'Supposing
she came to me, sensing that I'm uneasy,
singled me out for comfort and change of fortune';
yet know her poised contempt is all but certain.

Yes, like a brief sensation she goes by
and out of sight: why should she favour me
among so many strangers with sorrows, fears
like mine? I try to read—though feeling blurs
the glass of understanding time and again,
for all the will's concern to wipe it clean—

but look, she turns and springs, the logic gives
beneath her sudden weight! And now she curves
and ripples in my arm, her grappling claws
tear at my sleeve; the green uncanny eyes,
slotted with black, distil an arctic glare,
and endlessly her soft vibrating purr

winds intimacy off a reel of distance.
So she has come, indulging my pretence
of singularity and special need.
And let her now pretend my gratitude
in one final amused caress, before
I drop self-pity gently on the floor.

TIME FOR CLIPPING

On our arrival they were merely green
needles pricking the soil, with space between
for air and sunlight; pride of the previous owner,
who, dreaming a lawn quite innocent of weeds,

had cleared the ground, sprinkled the fine seeds
and left the rest to fate and gardener's honour.

For thirty weeks they grew undisciplined,
guzzling the rain and grappling with the wind;
each juicy filament took the lean and swerve
of its compacting wave in a churned lake.
At last, fetching the clippers and the rake,
I contemplate the sentence I must serve.

And then the blades move in, precise and swift,
chopping the tough lank fibres, and a drift
of shredded silk is loosed above the whish
and clack of the clean steel. In tangles wet
with hoarded rain—refusing to forget—
their fragrance lingers like a mindless wish.

At length we make our survey: sodden dirt,
a stubble grimed, uneven, but alert;
and there the slugs and earthworms that remain
through all retrenchments. Yet no real weed
is trundled out of consciousness to feed
the slow impartial bonfire down the lane.

POET ON THE BRINK

Calm autumn night, seen from a high window.
Above the roofs, the trees, an urban sky
breathed-on and fogged with light; a notched horizon
printed black; spread behind leaves, transparent
fans of lamp-gold; a clock-tower, white as bone,
rapt in a floodlit trance; and over all
a gritty hush, a solvent monotone.

The clock strikes peace—and any moment now
West 3 will beg a sonnet. Just remember
what's going on down there, and let it beg.
Most certainly the very houses seem,
and all that mighty heart is lying—still.
Even amid such trees the fluting owl
glides velvet through the darkness to his kill.

THE SWAN

Nothing more serene than the fluid neck,
the body curved like snow on foliage,
and spilt reflection moving smooth as oil.

But something wrecks the tranquil certainty:
the clean-cut shape unfolds; an evil wind
tears its roots out of the fertile water.

The pattern's tugged awry—the neck rammed stiff,
cumbrous wings whacking the startled air—
and terror swirls the surface of the lake.

THE WOODS

1

Semi-detached—how nice; with tiny gardens;
the paint so fresh and clean, the hedges trim.
Well-mannered avenues epitomise
the best of civilisation, don't you think?
Say, orderliness combined with charm and comfort.

> Perhaps. But notice especially the way
> the little roads end where the woods begin.
> A scarp of leaves towering above the rooftops
> completes the emblem, points the paradox
> of alienation and affinity.
> Nature endures, if only in the background.

How right you are. Men turn for sanctuary
to green retreats like this, as though to some
residual innocence deep down in the mind.

> That wasn't—

May I see what it's like in there?
So peaceful and inviting. And so romantic!
Someone told me this was Dick Turpin country.

2

How dim and cool it is; and very quiet.

People remove their talk, but not their litter.
And why they have to use a woodland stream
to dump their scrap-iron in, I can't imagine.
Isn't the water *foul.* It's hardly moving.

But just look at those trees. I love the way
their nets of foliage sieve the powdered sunlight.

For me there's something slightly ominous
in vegetable life so still and massive.
Do you remember how in fairy tales
the witches lived in woods?

Well yes—of course
I see what you mean. Yet, when all's said and done,
the trees are neutral: it is we ourselves—

At the weekends, and on bank holidays,
I'm told, this place is full of daring couples—

Where else could young love find, *à la belle étoile,*
freedom so nicely blended with seclusion?

—and swarms with peeping toms. You mentioned freedom:
ten yards from here a girl was raped and strangled.
They found her sprawling in a pool of mud.

How horrible.

And this is where the schoolboys
attacked the birds, destroyed their eggs, and stuck
pins through the heads of fledglings.

No, please don't.
I think we'd better go.

All right—but don't
go that way, if you're wise. There's something nasty
around the corner, dangling from a twig.
It's been on view a fortnight. Some young lover
left it, no doubt, to celebrate his manhood.

3

'Orderliness combined with charm and comfort'
I think you said? The woods, as we remarked,
complete the fable. And when I see a man
like that one, for example, with his paint-brush,

or that one with his shears clipping the hedge,
I am reminded of the untrimmed thickets
his peeping thoughts frequent. And of the pins
jabbing behind the laughter of his children.

SEEING PARKLAND FROM A CITY TRAIN

There's no going back, even if we were sure
    those origins are more than fanciful,
to green retreats where human life was pure.
But where was that clean break to justify
    schemes that would make an alien of nature?
Though Yeats's golden bird disowns the sky,
the goldsmith is no clockwork curio;
    being inventor, typifies the race
whose fate was not to abandon, but outgrow.
As lively sons and daughters, growing beyond
    (and celebrating thus) their parents' skill,
acknowledge all the same a family bond
by giving their affection and esteem,
    so it is good to prize what man constructs—
the hub of glass that swings the lighthouse beam,
the alert control tower and the viaduct—
    rejecting only what was made to please
some enterprising ape whose avarice mucked
communities and landscapes by the score;
    yet good, while praising these, to recognise
the long continuum that goes before,
linking inventive mind, emotion, sense,
    to primal mystery. And we're right to dream,
when brain and limbs have earned their indolence
working from what we know and can control,
    into the mind's vaguer distances—
but sift the inklings from the rigmarole
deadly with large oracular pretensions,
    for nothing is in focus at that range.
At least we learn by this our own dimensions;
the goldsmith cannot make a universe.
    To set beside the leisured eloquence
of water, branch and foliage, the terse
comment of glass and steel, is natural.
    And seeing those city dwellers in the park
I envy them their ease, and wish them well.

THE PAY IS GOOD

A class of thirty student engineers,
sixteen years old, disliked by all the staff.
Hearing about them at the interview,
and told to rule them with a rod of iron,
I tried my best but found I could not laugh.

He might be wrong. But I, no raw recruit,
had found a proverb in a classroom war:
the peaceful sheriff proves that he can shoot
before he throws his gunbelt on the floor.

A month or so of brooding self-distrust,
and then the moment came. I reached the door
(So this is it. Fight, for the love of Kell.
Show them who's boss—there's no going back—you must)—
and flung it open on the core of hell.

Somehow it worked. And they will never know
by what dissimulation it was done;
or how the fuse of terror blasted out
courage enough to master thirty-one.

ODE IN MEMORY OF JEAN FRANÇOIS GRAVELET, CALLED BLONDIN

What do we think now of the Seven Natural Wonders!
Niagara has nothing to match your skill:
that huge splayed energy is inept as fat
beside the strength whose terse and accurate jets
could thread the eyes of needles. We have no comment
equal to the occasion. More eloquent of amazement
the questions we should ask, though half suspecting
you would evade them, blind our understanding
with coloured flares of esoteric wisdom.

Are you exempt from fear, never to flinch
knowing that a second from now your foot may skid,
or a twitch of wind sway you the final fraction
into the arc of death? Are you superconscious,
quick as a turning diamond in the minute
adjustments of your artistry—or entranced
and vested with infallibility
like the somnambulist on the windowsill?—

unaware of sunlight and cool air
and steamboats holding their breath; of multitudes
legendary and silent attending miracles;
and drumming water, a precipice of foam
crumbling away like dynamited chalk.

I think that you would laugh and say our minds
were fluffy and whimsical; that your manoeuvres
derive from no arcanum, but demonstrate
a rational and lucid gaiety.
So you extemporise on homely themes—
trundle a wheelbarrow, bundle yourself in a sack,
stalk on a pair of stilts; and to clinch the matter
you cook us an omelette and lower it onto a steamboat.

Ten thousand taut stares, and you poised at their vertex!
Puppet-master, gentle, omnipotent,
you hold us by those lightly tugging strings.
Like a dramatic chorus you present us
exposed to one momentous circumstance,
delineating man's complexity.
Let us admit the craving for sensation
and orgies of vicarious adventure;
the envy sizing up your power and pride;
even the sense of horror that would suck
a curious pleasure from catastrophe.
And yet, a moment after you had fallen,
we'd wish to see you saved and reinstated.
Above all else we praise and cherish you
as steel-and-flint would praise the thunderstorm:
your lightning is the splendid thrust that makes
a laughing-stock of death; we hit and run.

Showman you are, daredevil, virtuoso,
greedy (who knows?) for money and applause.
These things we take for granted, but as part
and parcel of your genius.
The casual prodigies that you perform
are not explained by motives so banal:
mere egotism had safer ways to choose;
only vocation could afford to take
those skyhigh risks, and then to ask from danger
and skill's decisive act a pure delight.
Almost we see you fashioned for a strange
provoking destiny: to celebrate,
by your most delicate and courageous art,
the clarity that blurs with routine boredom,
all grace and daring dreamed but unachieved.

I wish you the best of luck. May you tread your nimble highway
a thousand times and live your seventy years.
And may you die in your bed of a bad cold, confounding
the owl-wise oracles who have called you fool.

CITADELS

That king spent fifty years or more
holding the devil at bay;
work was another name for war;
but then, growing grey,
he withdrew his men,
thought the devil would scarcely
trouble him again
since they had fought so fiercely.
And in no time the enemy
came swarming fresh from Hades,
quietly took the city
and raped the golden ladies.

This one at the first surprise
let the invaders in,
allowed them to swank and fraternise
and soak themselves with gin;
and when they stank with pleasure,
revealed at their most ghoulish,
gravely took their measure
and found them rather foolish.
Disarmed them while they snored,
prodded them back to Hades,
and feeling never so bored
returned to his golden ladies.

GOING ANYWHERE?

The limousine that Mr L.S. Dee,
tortured with ulcers and insomnia,
works like a slave to earn enough to run,
is indispensably related to
his job of marketing accessories
for the equipment used in setting up
the plant essential to producers of

an automatic measuring device
particularly favoured by those firms
that specialise in intricate machines
for companies that make a certain type
of electronic instrument designed
to regulate a mechanism required
by factories that supply materials
used in the shaping of precision tools
connected with the processes involved
in manufacturing refrigerators:
cold comfort for such perishable foods
as now enrich the breakfast Mr Grim
savours without conviction, being sick
from an anxiety neurosis due
to his employment in the firm that made
the limousine that Mr L.S. Dee,
tortured with ulcers and insomnia,
works like a slave to earn enough to run ...

FINE FRENZY

The opening draft's injected by the muse—
her medium, while entranced, being soft and porous.
She dries him then. He starts to pick and choose,
bashing the daylights out of his thesaurus.

Perhaps. And yet, if muses are divine
and poets all too human, why the hell
do opening drafts turn out so asinine,
while poems read superlatively well?

The medium is too earthy? That's fallacious,
for *Kubla Khan* came through without a hitch.
When trances are profound the muse is gracious,
but when they're shallow she's a perfect bitch.

No matter. Let the mind be dry or sopping,
it's still the finished product that's admired.
A line that cost the poet five days' chopping,
in fifty years will be his most Inspired.

DIFFERENCES
(1969)

DREAMS: A SEQUENCE

I
ARCHES

Arches on land,
half-circles only,
might dream
of what they miss.

And yet to stand
in a dark stream,
is this
not twice as lonely?

II
THE WOMAN

She makes no sound, no gesture;
grave and lovely in her long silk
stands waiting, and seems to understand
all that is dark to me. I draw the sword:
it glides a thread of steel across her lips,
perfecting silence. I regret
something I know must be—but it will end,
and she endure calmly.

The blade glints lethal now
to rob the prancing athlete of his head:
though he crouch wary, knife concealed,
he is no match for me. With naked breasts
the woman sits alone in her compartment.
The train moves, and we run elated—
killer and victim, two in one: myself—
effortless where she goes.

III
THE CITY

My feet slithered in mud, mashed
a lane's end slurring on the brink
of light and water. Evening shone low
its round of amber, turning pink
the clouds' edges and the snow.
The swirling river flashed.

And clear on the far side
arose the dream's manhattan, built

in piercing blocks of topaz, ruby, jade,
whose facets gleamed, whose windows spilt
unearthly light, and in my heart made
such happiness that I cried.

IV
OPPRESSORS

I lie in fever, delirious. The dark bedroom
winces under the silver whip of lightning.

I write my name, my prayer for heaven's mercy,
in ropes of green smoke on the brimstone air.

Across the neat advertisements in the paper
one large and arrogant stamps itself blood-red.

The teacher says we are here to learn Egyptian:
I ask him why the hell he is talking Greek.

He drags me out to beat me. I grab, exultant.
The metre stick lands *crack* on his hardboiled head.

V
THE MOUNTAIN

Through the still dark I walk alone
before the moon's rising. Small winds sigh
    on grassy slopes and cliffs of stone.
Hilltops are printed black against the sky.

    A gold thorn lifts behind a spur,
grows to a radiant crest that cleaves the night,
    and shines full mountain then, whose fur
is glowing wheat, is acres of combed light.

VI
THE DEDICATION

I too was in the choir. Imagine!—thousands
perching along the cliffs, and then the slow
chorale descending where the water shone
at break of day. How happily alike
the music and the sea's adagio—
for we were singing to the god Poseidon.

But when the hymn was over, one by one
the singers offered prayers of dedication

and then sat down. I thought 'How very odd
that they should use this drear monastic lingo,
clammy with guilt and self-humiliation,
to honour so exuberant a god.'

The bishop then (whose cassock sheathed him snugly
against the wind and spray): *We come to thee
with contrite spirits* ... 'But the god is gay!'
my heart protested. 'How can they not feel
the salt barbaric splendour of the sea!'
I stood there like a rock. I would not pray.

VII
FIRST LIGHT

The sun rises: dark
melts from tall buildings
    and leafy park

where a strange creature pads
whose fur is green moss
    whose form the leopard's

and trees drink deep
the quintessential calm
    of more than sleep.

VIII
THE TOWER AND THE OCEAN

To feel the wind up there
purling on those great battlements, I entered
the numb and stony darkness, and began to
trudge the coiled stair.

Heard, half way up, the sound
of scrubbing-brush and pail, where Mrs Crone
worked her poor fingers to the bone
in her long daily round.

The steps were hard and cold
on which she knelt, plying her only skill
year after year, and talking gaily still
though tired and old.

No stir of life but hers. On the top floor,
roneo, box-file, desk and balance sheet
furnished a room impersonal and neat
beyond an open door.

I turned to climb—above me the sweet air,
the final twist of stone. The way was barred,
and in black letters on a card
Not Open to the Public printed there.

A loophole shone in darkness: down below,
the tennis balls were soaring, floating, and
the players reaching up in a big wind.
Their rippling tunics dazzled me like snow.

And mounds of sapphire, flaring into white,
drowned half the sky in waves
whose crumbling scarps and luminous glissades
filled all my veins with light.

SMALL MERCIES

Someone ruled lines on a page of land
    with the railway for a margin,
and stuck the houses there in tidy rows.
Back to back or front to front, they stand
    aligned, allied, glaring
with tolerant hatred out of veiled windows.

But we are lucky, being in the end house
    of the first terrace. The back
enjoys the ramshackle remnant of a farm
turned coalyard, a meadow shared by an old horse
    and a lorry no one uses,
a tree with a night-owl hooting on its arm.

The end, of course, enjoys not being mean,
    and having its douse of air,
its glimpse of cherry branches on sky, its muddy
lane—reminds you of search and thrust, clean
    splitting, the point of vision:
headlands, the bows of ships, a man's love ready.

THE STRANGER

With ticking stick and boots like burst pods,
a long black overcoat and a withered hat,

a hunched hobo shuffles in our blind alley
  and sings in a loud voice.

Aria, dirge, chorale—or could it be
his own crude making? The words dissolve in wind;
only the music's warped adagio
  blares confidence in something.

And sets me wondering what weird compulsion
prods him along this road on a cramped Sunday—
the houses deadpan, the people shut away,
  not even a dog barking.

Insanity? A noisy camouflage
for a burglar quiet as a draught? Intoxication?
A drifter down on his luck. I'll give him the cash
  he needs because he needs it.

Diminuendo. I wait for him to return
doing his round of knocking. The singing stops.
He passes again, glaring from right to left ...
  Has gone, without a sound.

And leaves me free to imagine him possessed:
that suddenly—learning of death perhaps—
he knew what he had to sing to this dead end
  in one candescent stanza.

God knows what he was at: I'm none the wiser.
But feel his ghost haunting my ear, and wish
that all of us could sing in our blind alleys
  with such a clear madness.

MICROCOSM

As a small wilderness
the vegetable patch
declares its worth:
let loose, the children scratch
in hollows of dried earth,
bounce on a plank, or watch
the insects in the grass,
their bodies edged with light,
the tall weeds luminous.

No more than we deserve:
they to be left alone
to play, and I to work
in this clean living-room
their mother keeps so well:
routines we may not shirk
or barely stay alive;
with skill we buy the freedom
that disciplines our skill.

Too young to think it out,
how could they know that we
who sometimes nag and shout
are free when they are free,
clear of the mean restraint
grafted in all of us:
'Keep out of range,' I'd say,
'let me be generous'—
and they'd wonder what I meant.

JAZZ BOAT

The whispering roar of jets going over, tear-
ing slowly a sheet of silence. Clicking tongues
round mud and roots. A coolness in the air.
Where houseboats lull, a lamp's reflected light
on supple darkness floats its golden rungs.
Watching their movement in a cold black frame
of leaves, I think of Asmodeus' flight,
and fury settling as a dry despair.
There's no way out, and no one is to blame.
Then, sharp and sweet, a sound of jazz begins
to flirt across the Thames, the pleasure boat
shines in her glass.—Slowly the music thins,
the flake of light dissolves, and a small flame
that lilted in me falters and goes out.

PLAIN HUMAN

Up on this ladder, for instance,
scratching the paint away:
for what good reason? I ask myself
day after day.

Unless I maintain this property,
seal it, renew its gloss,
it can only deteriorate
and sell at a loss.

This is important because
I've a wife and kids to support,
and they're the last people in the world
I'd wish to hurt.

I'll feed, clothe, educate;
my children in turn will marry,
learn how to wait, and go up ladders,
and scratch and worry—

so that they will be able
to feed, clothe, educate
their children, who in turn will marry
and learn to wait,

and go up ladders, of course,
and scratch and worry, so that ...
Day after day I ask myself
precisely what

this worry-go-round is meant for;
and sometimes I look out
at the garden, which is a wilderness,
and I am caught

in a small calm of seeing:
the dustbin, perhaps, tilted
under trees at the broken fence,
light spilt

through leaves, a crimson flower
floated on air: alive
and clear in reciprocal stillnesses.
And what they have—

or what I give them, or
begin to share with them—
has nothing to do, it seems, with use
or beauty or emblem:

something to do with being
themselves. And I become
the dreamer full of discontent,
who thinks of wisdom,

solitudes, mysteries, lives
of prophets, obscure books;
the child who loved sunsets (I'm told)
and wistful nooks;

or the student who wasted time
on unprescribed authors
like Swedenborg, Boehme, the Eastern sages,
the Church Fathers;

who lagged in green retreats
to watch the mind's horizon,
or prowled the neon maze when love
secreted poison.

I have grown up since then.
Or have I? If other people
delight in working from nine to five,
are thrilled to grapple

with mortgage and hire purchase,
if it overflows the cup
of happiness to own a car,
and that's *grown up*,

well, I am still a child.
Or one of the stubborn fools
who keep on asking why and whither,
subjecting rules

to scrutiny, slipping custom.
One who can sympathise
with bums on benches, Beats on beaches
dancing to jazz,

sleeping in caves and boxes,
living on fish, avoiding
work, marrying (no strings attached)
merely by wading

into the pristine sea—
but finally aimless, caught
on the hook of the old question, flapping
like fish out of water.

'Maybe it's not the place
that matters, nor what you do,'
the dreamer in me says, 'nor simply
a point of view,

but seeing, in the light
of the last analysis,
that this—the flower, the world—is so
because it's this.

Where faith coagulates,
the fears and problems tease:
we carry the why inside us
like a disease.'

Bravo: being semi-detached
instructs you how to see
hunchback and cancer victim,
beggar and refugee;

to bless the praying-mantis
munching her lover's head,
the atman of the torture cell
and the launching pad.

Figment or godlike vision,
being single it must fail
all but the crank and sage,
or petrify the will.

Plain human, I prospect
in rocky streams: let sand
bring crumbs at random, fine inklings of gold
to the weathered hand.

MUSIC

Do I believe in marriage?
If you mean what I think you mean,
the answer must be no—
no more than I value any convention
except for its convenience.

I think the universe is
a formal creation like music,
patterns within patterns,
and that we try instinctively
to bind our own notes together:
from atoms of sound to make molecules;
from molecules, cells ...

The bonding for social patterns is
love's valence if you're lucky,
and if you're not, affection,
pity, tolerance, justice.

Institutions are merely
names, and the names a way
of saying what people tried,
and of making rules
that first describe and then
demand the repetition of
what seemed to work best:
the man and woman bound
to their own offspring,
the dominant seventh to
the tonic triad.

But the rule-makers are always
catching up, consolidating—
after Beethoven comes
Debussy, and then Schönberg,

breaking away, creating—
and in different countries
harmonic systems differ.
So with the norms for marriage, procreation,
the bringing-up of children.

I don't believe in marriage, a mere name:
I believe in staying with
my mate and children
as long as they need or want me,
from a love or what you will
whose counterparts unite
atoms in molecules
or tones in triads—
making a social music.
Though doing it desperately
while the other half
of a double destiny loosens
the universe, and all that's made
suffers a slow corrosion.

LEGENDS: A SEQUENCE

I
STANDING WATER

Ironist now, equilibrist, I was
a hero then—the salt a sailor's wit,
a winedark leaping lustre, supple, taut,
spuming beneath the wind; and heroes' laws
were elemental rhythm—no human thought
to clip the dream, to make the passion fit.
I used to marvel as I watched the ship
slicing luminous fathoms: she would dip
and rise, alive and shuddering on a will
that chose the meaning for her, by dominion
freed her from the exigencies of freedom—
its power, acknowledged, then most prodigal.

Agents of destiny, we chose the means
but not the meaning: primal opposites
involved us in their greatness as we manned
the fateful seesaw. Now, both rise
and fall forsake me. Landlubber, prudent king,
diplomat, man of means, with time to think,
compelled to choose a meaning I devise
these ironies that bring
contraries into temper: choose, in fact,
the mean—for we are human. This is not
despair, extremity—since rise and fall
forsake me now: when life and death contract,
when water stands, both are impossible.
This mood is but the fog and stink of meanness,
miasma of the deadlife, meaning's rot.

II
WOUNDS

A blank, like this.
Fog muffling the shore,
a tedium of sand,
the trite conforming pebbles.
Only the sea's hiss
reminds me of its roar.
A salt memory troubles
wounds that will not heal.
The spent wave whispers
Odysseus, now you feel
the salt rubbed in, the lost

leap of the sea transmuted.
Who sailed to islands, kissed
Calypso once, and knew
the taste of salt leaping,
safe in his kingdom drew
a blank, a wet mist
on grey shingle weeping.

III
CALYPSO

Crazed by the suck and roar
of spinning water—nine days
clear of the drowned—tugged from a lurching spar,
flopped like a seal where waves elide and glaze
warm sand, I came ashore.
The sailor found his woman standing there.

Firelight on hair and skin; a scent
of smoke from cedar logs and pepperwood.
She called me and I went,
making no choice of bad or good:
whatever choosing meant,
only the girl, half goddess, understood.

The coiled sea takes us in.
Freeing ourselves we bind ourselves:
doing what we need, we do what must be done.
The cone of darkness fills as it revolves,
lifts us out into the foaming sun.
Climactic water swills the jagged shelves.

The crusts of fire flake down: a red spark
dissolves in moonlight ... Dawn, the slow
focusing of rock where four streams play
beneath a vine; deep woods for owl and crow,
clear of the filtered dark.
A trance of distance sublimates the bay

to a thin sift of thunder ...
After such nights, such days. At first,
leaving her there asleep, I used to wander
back to the crude source, where combers burst
spilling white grains of water,
and squealing gulls—touched nerves in the wind—

were twinges of sharp lust.
Both day and night, it seemed, were provident,

reciprocal as host and guest.
And yet the idyll faltered, the enchantment
left something over, grit of discontent:
the innocence of dawn became a cyst.

Hunched in the cool dark one afternoon,
I heard Calypso singing while she wove—
her body, in the opening of the cave,
edged with a down of light. Perhaps the tune,
the blonde hair brimming over in the sun,
a movement, or some old domestic flavour

tricked me—or indeed
I solved an absence by telepathy,
from the deep shafts of truth a slighted need
drew substance: but I saw Penelope
there, in an arched radiance, and she made
from whispering spools a web of loyalty.

The dour eroding pain
grown harsh, I left the cave,
clambered through wind that sawed against the grain
of gnarled blue water; in the grumbling cove
loitered all afternoon,
hearing the shingle rasp, the gulls complain.

Perhaps desire and guilt
grinding together, or the lie
that strikes through self-fulfilment, a rock's fault.
On jagged shelves the leaping foam gives way
in slack pools, finally in grains, a dry
precipitate, the irony of salt.

IV
THE WEB

Alone under the sky, the horizon our only limit—
never limiting but always moving away, granting
something to move towards, and space to move in
that never stopped being distance until the skyline
was rock that stayed put (though landfall meant
freedom too, actions worth travelling for)—
we were the few for whom the sea was woven.

I stand now on the cliffs on a summer day.
White clouds accumulate above the horizon,
whose tempered edge stays put, and bounds a space
empty of ships. With a pretence of meaning

the water glides towards me in shining folds—
is chafed and slashed, ravels on black stone.
There is no meaning here: I have none to give.

My home, my island kingdom: in bays and inlets
the spent sea scuffs, kicking the driftwood idly.
I climb through drowsy air: voices of bee and cricket
float on the gulls' cries. In a nest of bracken
I see a silky cone, as though a tunnel
of spun smoke, delicate and exact—
and deep inside, patient as death, the spider.

V
SPECIAL PLEADING

Even now, so long after my return,
she weeps despairingly some days, thinking
of how the past violated the future,
trying to understand. For me, in a sense,
there was nothing to understand but being a man
who voyages far from home, elate with searching;
but nothing I say dissolves her metaphor
of the needling worm, the fruit brown and pulpy
losing its grip. She attacks, and pity grows
a steel point of guilt: in self-defence
I stab, and then regret. The killer's love
makes murder suicide. And not to die—
sailor at heart, sickening of government—
I plead there are salt reaches woven, unravelled,
woven again by the world's generous rhythm;
and proud sorrowful hands unpicking truth
for virtue's sake, craftily, night by night.

VI
GRASS WIDOW

'Can you imagine what it did to me,
that long torment of belief and doubt?—
how I grew sick of drudging day and night,
of lying alone, watching the blank sea,
hearing the drunken suitors brag and fight,
afraid some bitch would let the secret out.

P for Penelope, and pure, and prude:
the choice of words could sting, but made known
the speaker's heart, not mine. How many read
truly the cipher of my solitude?
Which of them would have fondled me in bed
to give me pleasure, not to steal a throne?

I was not pure, nor prudish: there were nights
I longed to do what other women do,
afflicted with a sweet insanity
that fashioned gods even from parasites.
It wasn't fear, or shame, or vanity
restrained me then, but somehow, loving you.'

VII
UP TO A POINT

How are we different then?
If this is Love
that pairs a wife with other men
in fancy, but in deed
preserves her for a husband's need—
as though a glove

could fit no hand but one—
Love is too dim
to understand what men have done:
I'd rather hear you say
we're friends, lascivious and gay:
let's pension him.

And then the way is clear
to wonder why
your will, if not in shame or fear,
could hold, and mine slip
like driftwood from the weir's lip,
no longer I.

What makes a man destroy
all gentle thought,
turn killer in the streets of Troy
or sweat in Circe's bed?
Self-will, the moralists have said;
but I have caught

a stranger meaning there:
that when the will
pierces to remote air,
ascending like a stone
whose arc implies how it was thrown,
it soars until

an infinitely small
articulation
ease its thrusting to a fall.

Dark causes that direct
self-will, accomplish their effect
by self-negation.

What cloth can match the weave
of right and wrong?
Hurled stones—you felt in make-believe
a lover's hands, and I
was drawn like any traveller by
Calypso's song.

But somehow you were still
yourself—had stopped
in time the soaring thrust of will—
when mine had reached the crest
and touched a needle point of rest
before it dropped.

VIII
THE SINGERS

The logs crack and flare.
Each night the storytellers dream
and lightly
pluck their harps and sing,
praising a wife's care,
a fearless king.
And we who are their theme
listen politely.

Deceivers who have no
alternative, we let the myth
grow stronger.
The divided air
resumed its single flow,
but now we share
what death has tampered with,
a love no longer

filling canvas, fresh
with salt. Hearing the words float
on wonder,
trying to know the god
grained in the mortal flesh,
you see blood
spurt from a slashed throat,
and rape, and plunder;

spent killers after war
hungry for sex, grown tired of ships
and danger,
debauched in some glazed island
by drug peddler and whore;
the wasting husband,
new salt upon his lips,
come home a stranger.

What lies they tell to make
ideal truth! No false relations
tangle
this music combed from harps,
though women lie awake
and love warps,
and partners sworn to patience
fret and wrangle.

Heroic tempers brood
in the after-calm, as sultry air
forebodes
violence. We have no
healing from solitude
when in the slow
acid of your despair
a dream corrodes.

IX
DREAM AND REALITY

In the estuary the fresh and the salt mingle.
Her supple calms beneath the noon sun
glide on shingle, flicker with thorned light.
In a translucent haze, bulged waters run
smoothly between the headlands.—Not where grinding
fathoms crumble the bones of lost ships,
or clinking brooks are winding amidst granite,
but where the markets hum and the galley dips
creaking along the wharf in a stink of tar,
life proves the grain of wisdom, and we learn
humanity. The spar, the drowned man, deep
in a groiling cone of violence, turn and turn:
in the spun pool of frenzy a hero's will
founders: whose rage cries out? whose arm jags
the blade home, swills the Trojan ground with blood?
But here men watch the tide: their net swags
its load of rinsed silver across the gunnel;
others bake bread, construct in marble, crush

the grape for sweet runnels of wine, fill
their water skins where cold shallows flush
on pebbles, dump cedar logs that cough
a golden spindrift under the fat cauldron,
lead cattle to the trough. Still lovers hate,
and parents fight an absurd war with children;
a rival is broken or a friend betrayed;
by misadventure, suicide, disease,
Death's fortune is made. The people curse
and weep and go on living: by degrees
the balance levels, tilts the other way
with dancing and making love and the pride of skill.
I've watched the numb grey of *meden agan*
burn as the golden mean when heart and will
have coupled. Residual passion stirs in dreams
and legends, from whose dark truth are drawn
blinding extremes that flare in the mind's mirror
but, freed from distance, outrage human law—
rive the tough grain, leaving it scorched and brittle.
Alone in the noon silence I look down
at the estuary, the little streets and buildings,
the sea cutting blue notches in the town—
inland the glancing torrents and the groves,
and where the waves pound, headlands dividing
gull-flaked coves, thinning away like echoes,
and heaped with immense clouds the ocean sliding
godly across the world: calm vision makes
one harmony of the disparate, but we live
where wholeness breaks, where objects, qualities,
beliefs and feelings are competitive—
but then defined reciprocally, as though
a kind of love made difference possible,
or difference a kind of love. And we grow human
where opposites are poised, made workable,
where salt and fresh merge at the river's end.
The task of hermit or of hero feeds
on energies that transcend the human will,
yet has for origin the same needs
as those that keep this little town alert,
edgy, tenacious—where, though difference
intensified can hurt, becoming conflict,
passion releases no such violence
as ravaged in the howling streets of Troy.
But black shadows are made by brilliant light:
deep joy involves deep sorrow, people say,
remembering those whose fortune was to fight
human tyranny, natural disaster—
festering heroes, layabouts, war bores

bogged in the past, drinking themselves to death.
Yet many have come to terms, outgrown the whores
in foreign seaports, camaraderie, total
discipline that absolved them from the need
to think, and the brutal ecstasy of killing:
these are the ones I search—not those who bleed
memories in the pubs—for signs of pain,
and then of joy: veterans who came home
and took the strain of being entirely human.
In firelight the harp glissandos run like foam
from bows that slice green water: I watch the eyes
dreaming, think how the floated words tell
true lies, shaping, distancing all that lures
the mind to make a fact of heaven or hell—
difference intensified, the fresh and salt
unmingled, hero's rage and hermit's trance.
A rock's fault ... Slowly the wound heals,
the severed strata knit: and in the glance
of women who for parched years were still
themselves, grass-widowed while their husbands learned
to gallivant and kill, experience lights
a penetrating love, where the old burned
wistful in bland wax. My dreams contain
the truth of primal opposites; in the common
I find their strong blend, the truly sane:
Penelope and Calypso in one woman.

FREUD

When did you hear me say
'Now that you know
what forces are at play,
you must let go,
and on the dark tide
of a violent age
drift into suicide'?

I did not teach despair,
but how it could be defeated
by fact and order. Beware
the cry of the Zeitgeist-monger;
all history can swerve
to the pull of one man's hunger—
and sick minds can be treated.

GOSPEL TOWN

Under its hump the town
endures nightfall. Sand
sweats as the tide uncovers
drainage and slimy stone.
Fairylights, fountain, bandstand
play the uneasy lovers.

Their ingrown hungers rage:
hot sermons, anodyne
of hymns, disturb the patter
of the hypnotist on the stage,
where tranced lips guzzle wine
from glasses filled with water.

Pure streams from granite ledges
fall through the glens, and swill
flat shingle solitudes
beyond the last bridges.
Unfathomably still
the black mountain broods.

THE UNDERTOW

What is it sets the alarm
to drill me at six-thirty,
impels me away from home
and across the city,
defined by the suit I keep
for occasions? What is it tries
to drag me back to sleep,
dulling my eyes,
wanting the other to steer
clear and leave me alone?
Why do I turn the fear
to a skin of ice, a stone
crust on the quick of magma?
I arrive at a box of glass
as cold as dogma;
no whisper of trees, no grass:
man is the spearhead now.
What thrusts me into this room
where they offer no welcome, bow
over documents, exhume
my past, rummage and prod,

shoot questions at me like
a firing squad,
or turn me on a spike
over their singeing scorn?
'Thank you' ... In the street
I feel my roots torn
for building, am obsolete
as greenness. But trees rejoice—
not I: before I started
something had made a choice
and left me heavy-hearted,
reluctant, turning in.
Survival says I should be
content to have saved my skin—
licking my wounds, but free
of the specialists branching towards
extinction: the one who found
his hands and a gift for words.
But I wince at the drilling sound:
it jags in me like a knife.
You tried the flowers, the birds,
the gnat and the dinosaur:
which candidate now, dear life?
Where are you heading for?

OPEN TO THE PUBLIC

After four centuries—from the dirt
grand patrons dwindled to—merchants and plebs
reverse their destiny at the clicking stile.
Into an ancient calm the children blurt,
where leisured paths wander and cattle graze.
The lake prickles with sunlight, and a mile
of foliage cools the summer in green webs.

The mansion from its legendary haze
emerges hard and white. Respectful clods,
we climb the steps, enter the Great Hall.
Hushed voices echo; a subtle brilliance plays
on bronze and marble. Eros and Apollo,
immured with Cicero and the Dying Gaul,
are stone-cold dreams who once were living gods.

Adagio from room to room we follow
the guidebook through an intricate décor

of gold and peacock, walnut, stucco, silk.
Some say magnificent, and others hollow;
a few say Robert Adam and look wise.
The youngsters grouch, a baby squalls for milk;
two schoolboys, tired of art, are playing war.

This grandeur was a politician's prize,
its history laced with blood. First Somerset,
then Simple Tom the Martyr, lost their heads,
and Cruel Henry in a warp of spies
coughed on a musket ball. Here Cromwell honed
the steel that left a monarchy in shreds,
and love turned violent in a widow's net.

Death claimed his revenue, the proud atoned
for daring to possess; then duke and duchess,
marrying peace and comfort with renown,
were free to cherish gaily what they owned—
had pipers and Swiss porters, worked the land,
renewed a structure and a style, till Brown
and Adam put the last beguiling touches:

where lilies float, two lovers hand in hand
gaze on the water they are pictured in,
and dark things are transfigured as they were
when blades and virgins danced the saraband.
Softly the polished ivy hugs the tree,
the belladonna makes a drowsy stir,
and a clear sky dissolves the peregrine.

At the old riding-school they serve a tea
of buttered toast and scones and cherry cake.
Sparrows from airy rafters dive for crumbs,
a royal coach displays its pedigree:
and dilettanti calling up the past
omit the slopping guts, the mashed thumbs,
and courtly rascals mirrored in the lake.

The little patrons—raw, but learning fast—
retire and leave this glory to the dark.
In terraces and flats the pride of kings
inches like mercury: half iconoclast
and half creator, life through arc on arc
moves endlessly—and leaves among the things
it lavished at the crest, this lovely park.

FIVE FOOT TEN

Among the drooping plants
a few green hairs
on a dry scalp of mud
itchy with ants,
their trickling multitude
busy with great affairs.

Each tiny street
fidgets and effervesces
with two-way traffic. They meet
head on, avoid with slick
footwork collision and loss.
But social stresses

erupt in frenzied wars:
they squirt and pinch
in twos and then in dozens,
their highways inch by inch
glutted with scores
of slaughtered citizens.

Inside a lens
only the scale alters:
proportion is the same
between intelligence
and the achieved aim.
A different need filters

pain and aspiration
into the crystal jars
of love and art and god,
whose distillation
spills from the smashed beauty
among the brains and blood.

One world, an equal right
to live, for ants and men.
One irony of *us*
or *them*: one need to fight.
They're small but numerous;
we're few, but five foot ten.

My life must act, being theirs.
Gigantic, swift, I raise
the kettle: they had their chances.
While that which makes me human—
my pitying heart—delays,
the lethal fluid pounces.

METAMORPHOSES

In blocks of serpentine
polished for generations
by families going down to Kynance Cove,
the coloured minerals tangle veins as fine
as threads, like intricate decorations.
Charmed by their loveliness,
the shine of August, waves on smooth sand,
how could we think of metamorphic stress,
of burning fluids that wove
the subtle characters we tread,
in whose complexities each delicate strand
shows how the earth bled—
or, among swimsuits, towels, suntan lotion,
slipping off shirts and frocks
where long ago magmatic waters drained,
and seeing the compulsive ocean
carve what those trickling fires engrained,
read our own birth and shaping in the rocks?

Mysterious fragments—so the cliff dreams—
shine on the littoral that was forming here
like a crude prototype of bone
when salty shallows coupling with the wind
conceived the biosphere:
with colours purer than its own—
a mineral vision dancing in the bay—
empyrean satin gleams
on bodies tender, golden-skinned,
that blur in bright obscurities of spray
and come forth radiant still.
But neither rock nor breaker shares
with man the double will
he seeks where only energies can be—
while a curt rubric on the tideline spells
changes as natural as theirs:
windless, the living fires go out, and cells
are broken down like crystals in the sea.

But who should think of death
on such a day, in such a place as this,
where everything perceived can be enjoyed?
Guests of the green ocean, drawing breath
from the same wind, and noticing perhaps
with what an easy grace two youngsters kiss,
white girl and coloured boy—how they avoid,
coming on truth instinctively, the traps

of superstition—we might have thought rather
that wholeness and diversity generate
the only love the world has ever known,
that differences belong to one another:
reciprocal the forms of cliff and sea,
the little points and lines flecking the stone,
the people and their races. But only we—
who feel distinctions, having minds and hearts—
can love, trying to see the whole, or hate,
insisting on the parts.

From sinuous intrusions
weaving the colours of the serpentine,
to the spun chromosomes prefiguring
the nerve cells of a son or daughter
delighted by a pebble, everything
is change: to make and to destroy
lose meaning in the rich confusions
of chance or infinite design.
And yet at Kynance Cove, seeing a boy
beaten against the cliff—but not by water:
by a man's will and sinew—
and thinking how the tide of kinship runs
compulsively, and of the neural stress
that sparks all human sorrows, angers, fears,
I wept for differences. In rage of guns
primordial fires continue:
but magma, though hell-hot, is passionless,
and the salt streams on rocks were never tears.

THE VETERAN

One of the lucky ones,
I do what I can.
Chatting, reading the news
to an old disabled man,
I wonder how
he stays in his right mind,
so much of his world is dead.
He faced the guns
at Ypres, was gassed and sent
to this very ward where now—
lacking his left eye,
in the other almost blind,
with an arm he cannot use,

legs damaged, a tube to drain
his bladder, a little bag
of urine at his thigh—
once more he sits in bed,
endures the long drag
of time without event,
the slow corrosive pain.

The first time he said 'sir',
hearing the way I spoke,
it made me wince, and then
it was touching and amusing—
as though I were
a young padre diffusing
good cheer among the men.
Being treated so, in view of
his eighty years and all
he'd seen of life and death,
was quite a joke.
Sometimes he would recall
the things I only knew of
from text or photograph,
and now the thin breath
that whistles in his throat,
the clouded eye, the grey
cadaverous face,
remind me every day
of how he bled
once in a remote
time, a remote place,
and has been living half
a century with the dead.

DOLORES
A little girl who survived a firing squad 32 years ago,
but who has been in a coma ever since, died today.
                              —Newspaper report, 1968

Thirty two years ago,
shifting the corpses for burial,
they found her underneath
still breathing.

The bullet drawn,
her delicate flesh made whole,

she slept through the long maturing
of child and maid and woman.

Her blood ran evenly, her brain
lived on when her mind stopped:
form without meaning,
a name for no one.

Lying alone
deep in the snarled growth
of rose and lily,
she had one gift at least:

if love, searching, torn
on briars, was almost there,
and would have kissed her wide awake
to the last blaze of childhood—

her mother's weeping,
her father's hard silence,
the dreadful intimation (worse
than nightmares or being lost)

when suddenly all the rifles
pointed one way, demanding
her four simple years—
she died before it reached her.

INTEGRATION

Suddenly I heard squeals
echoing under the bridge. Beside the water
a dog at his mistress' heels
came slouching. My little daughter
ran to the safety of my arm
and huddled there,
staring. 'He won't do you any harm'
I said. A moment later
it was my turn to stare.

A mongrel: its body a stodged
Alsatian, the head thickened;
its face, abrupt as a mask under
a sooty streak of hair, some kind
of terrier. Passing us, it dodged

furtively, long tail wilting, to skulk behind
protective legs. For a moment I felt sickened
as if by a cruel joke, or at best a blunder
due to an absent mind.

Yet mixtures are common enough:
in art, in people and animals, flowers and metals,
old jealousies compromise,
and unities die in the heterogeneous stuff
to make fresh unities. Custom smooths
a gravelling image: in the eyes
of the dazed beholder beauty settles,
as though a riddle were solved, or lies
turned themselves into truths.

The shock of novelty then.
Or could it be one of those
disparities that forever outrun
the stride of the human mind,
like the hippo bulking on tiny trotters, men
savaging what they love, or the sun
killing the root with kindness? Terrier's nose,
Alsatian's rump: to whoever, whatever designed
the multifarious world it is all one.

THE RIVER

The content of a river is
its form, its form the water
that is the river. The river is itself.
Not water simply,
but water folded, curled
exactly thus and now ... and now ... and now:
tugged smooth on clenched knuckles,
a skin of oiled light
sleeking off rock; the smash
of dumped foam; gold lenses over gravel.

Each detail is itself,
exactly here and now. Inventing space:
no edge of water fines to definition,
the split hair splits—but nowhere, being here,
masses and shines like water.
Inventing time: this now
was then—the split second

split to infinity—yet now or never
evolves the racing water,
whose planes are stillness gliding off a spool.

Each clear identity is so because
all are reciprocal: this rock, this water
not simply that, but rock being smoothed by water,
and water honed on rock.
But with no here and now, unless
everywhere, always: each immeasurable,
all therefore simply this. Without these shapes,
themselves, there is no river; without the river,
nothing. The river is the form,
the form the content. The content is itself.

PIGEONS

They paddle with staccato feet
in powder-pools of sunlight,
small blue busybodies
strutting like fat gentlemen
with hands clasped
under their swallowtail coats;
and as they stump about,
their heads like tiny hammers
tap at imaginary nails
in non-existent walls.

Elusive ghosts of sunshine
slither down the green gloss
of their necks an instant, and are gone.

Summer hangs drugged from sky to earth
in limpid fathoms of silence:
only warm dark dimples of sound
slide like slow bubbles
from the contented throats.

Raise a casual hand—
with one quick gust
they fountain into air.

1946

THE BROKEN CIRCLE
(1981)

SKY POEM

Taking off, he's glad of the rough power
    he has little use for: the towing plane
bullies both wind and spirit, but like a ripsaw
    slices along their grain.

At two thousand feet he drops the cable,
    feels the glider float free—
air sliding and whispering over wings
    like an ideal sea.

He plays off gravity against the surge of wind,
    moving the controls lightly to steer
uncalculated courses, true to the subtle
    weave of the atmosphere.

And knows the signs, the promises: where he sees
    a puff of cumulus he can soar
in slow circles on the rising heat.
    But nothing delights him more

than the unexpected gift of a blue thermal
    suddenly taking hold of the plane
in its long glide down, like a soft explosion
    urging it up again.

Sometimes, though, the sky turns sulky,
    withdraws her lithe and buoyant air:
the flier, for all his art, can only droop
    to a field in the middle of nowhere.

SKILLS

1

    It's sad when an old house goes,
and all that's left of a room is a crust of wall
with shreds of the dreamy paper someone chose
    to make her days less drab.
    Yet I love watching the bricks fall
    when the man in the caterpillaring cab
pulls a lever and swings a huge iron ball.
    I heard his mates in a pub
    one lunch hour, boasting that he could aim
his bullying missile finely enough to rub
    a matchstick into flame.

2

    Just look at the new erection!—
one of those monstrous cubes with a glib skin,
assuming an identity by reflection.
    But I saw a bricklayer there,
    grey-haired, haggard, aloof from the din
    of drills and engines, with infinite care
bringing a twist of wall to its odd perfection.
    My neighbour, watching too,
    called it, with scorn, the Collar. To me
its taut curve seemed beautiful and true,
    and the man who built it, free.

NATURAL SELECTION

No larger than the fingers
tweezing them out of nets,
they flip in jam jars—blunt faces
stubbed on windows, as though
their element had betrayed them,
turned glass, turned murderer.

'Let's watch them,' I suggest, 'see
what they look like, then throw them back
in the river where they belong.'
I point out circular eyes and pulsing mouths,
fins wavering in a liquid breeze,
and flecks of pearl lighting the brown bodies.

No one listens. 'I have more fish than you!'
'Yeah, but I've got one
that's bigger than any of yours!' The voices
clash till it's time to leave; and then the small
demanding humans give the small demanding
fish back to the river, the free for all.

THE NEIGHBOURHOOD

The sun's a damp stain in peeling grey.
    The terrace across the way
is porridge brown, spattered with pebble-dash.

The doors are black, the windows black and cream.
Each railing wears a chunky hedge, trim
  as a diplomat's moustache.

Gardens, this road is called: a cul-de-sac
  beside the railway track,
as fertile as a fridge. The small lives pause,
bemused and parenthetic, in a square
bracket of bricks and mortar, wondering where
  they lost the main clause.

Or, with no head for syntax, feel no loss:
  apply fresh coats of gloss,
drudge patiently six days, visit the pub
on Saturday night, sleep late on Sunday, gape
at the telly after lunch, read news of rape,
  or give the car a rub—

and glow with a dim contentment. Maybe so:
  who would pretend to know?
Myself, I watch the taut abstractions crumple,
the white light, splintered, make a coloured world.
Customs are single, neighbours manifold:
  I call no man 'a sample'.

Fred is a bus inspector, brisk and squat;
  fond of his garden plot,
TV, the *Daily Herald*, and keeping hens.
Smoked forty fags a day, then gave it up
with no more fuss than turning off a tap;
  and outraged commonsense

by trying philosophy in evening classes.
  We hear him as he passes—
heading for the allotment on his bike—
or damps a bonfire till it oozes smoke,
greeting our children with his cheerful squawk
  of *allow, luvly!*—like

a cockney parrot. Ada, his town-bred wife,
  thinks ours is country life,
and H—— unparalleled this side of heaven.
Gets up at six, works in a factory, stops
at twelve to clean and bake and visit shops;
  goes once a year to Devon,

sends us a postcard and a tin of cream;
  and spices her esteem

with love when we are good, with shy reproof
when ironies of travelling paint us naughty:
our baby-sitter, at eleven thirty,
    is martyred and aloof.

Then Mrs Mildew, stately and correct:
    her son, an architect,
preferred his freedom to her apple pie.
A close-up of her husband—from far off
an all-in wrestler (tired as well as tough)—
    one morning gave the lie:

his glance was mild blue light, a dream distilled:
    half child half adult, filled
with aching distances, I thought him then;
imagined frosty prudes—who polish brass
and judge creation through a pane of glass—
    refrigerating men.

The whole bright spectrum plays its colours here:
    Larry, an engineer,
is gentle, skilled, obliging, full of fun.
Meg chats and chuckles, with her brilliant stare.
The world should be well thrashed by Mrs Square.
    And Mr Watkinson,

a lanky introvert, reserved but genial,
    complete with pipe and spaniel,
a walk to match his educated speaking,
strides meditative through his broad demesne—
a strip of pavement and a scraggy lane.
    Poor Mrs Jawd is peeking—

her black eyes tortured, mouth oblique and thin,
    her nose a shark's fin—
to see what someone's up to. Mr Poole
fought, and is fighting still, the wicked Germans:
indoctrinates his son with martial sermons,
    then sends him to Sunday school.

Some go to church, some to the Citadel.
    Others would keep the bell
and damn the belfry. Half of them are back
where Moses managed, but without the gush
of sacred water and the burning bush:
    curled in their cul-de-sac.

But all of them 'suburban'? All the same?
    Contented, smug, tame?

A single road is opal in its moods.
And then you hear of one that went berserk;
of rape, and children kidnapped in the park,
    and death in Cranford Woods.

TRADITIONS

Last night was the last: today
the lorries and dormobiles
are ready to go, the dodgems are stowed away,
dive bombers and ferris wheels
are packed as neat as biscuits. Jack the Ripper
is roping canvas, Dracula's Daughter brings
the baby's wind up, and the stripper
(naughty but nice) is clearing the breakfast things.

Where children play in the sun,
under the lights the servants of the Lord
advanced their placards against the Evil One:
they wake to Sunday, the promise of their reward
bright for another spell. But rich and poor
are the points of reference here, not body and soul:
loud engines jam the larksong over the moor,
and the big trailers roll.

SABBATH TRIPTYCH

Music by Wagner: horns and violins
propose the condonation of his sins
who honoured God the Logos. Mr Smith
would rather have a car to tinker with,
a hedge to trim, and God the Mechanist—
aloof, the cosmos ticking on his wrist.
Between the radio and electric shears,
myself and two Jehovah's Witnesses
contending on the doorstep. 'It's all here
in black and white, the prophecies are clear'
they tell me, shaking dust off, snapping God
the Father in a briefcase. Overhead
the unclouded sunlight equably surveys
its colours redisposed a thousand ways.

DEFICIENT CAUSE

So *you* began the violence and the pain—
   with you the whole creation fell!
In place of Abel you were given Seth,
     but horror outlasted Cain.
The panther tore the heart from the gazelle
   and children starved to death.

Your sin was certainly original!
   Even Augustine, who believed
nothingness made you love the lesser good,
     was baffled by the Fall.
If you transgressed your nature, you achieved
   more than Jehovah could.

Making you perfect man he made you free—
   though what alternative you had
to choosing rightly, since your will was true,
     is difficult to see.
If something ('nothing'?) turned your good will bad,
   that wasn't willed by you.

Poor Adam. What the fossil record pleads,
   kinship is quick to grant. You learned,
as surely as the protozoic slime,
     to satisfy your needs.
That 'disobedience' was a fire that burned
   aeons before your time.

PORTRAITS

1

Grandpa, total abstainer and lay preacher,
worked in a Lisburn mill
and played his flute in the local band.
Outside the kitchen door, before breakfast,
singing hymns with a reedy old-man's voice,
he polished boots till they shone
like black glass in the frosty sunlight.
He wore an exact grey suit,
a watch-chain across his waistcoat,
a hat impeccably grooved and upright.

No memory of laughter, even
of smiling teeth: I recall a man who chuckled,
his lips merry under a chopped chunk
of bristles, the skin creasing
like soft leather around his eyes.

2

Grandmother called me 'son'. I remember her smile,
her warm contralto voice.
Gentle ascetic, she had worked her body
to a dry and seasoned spareness.
Looking back, I see
the simplicity that made
such calms of certitude and love.
What glowing angers too, when she was younger,
must have left burn-marks on
the characters of her children.

My father had her eyes. So had the hero
of his most dramatic sermon,
who stormed into the temple
and sent crashing from up-ended boards
an avalanche of silver.

BROTHERLY LOVE

My people brought them the Word in a new guise,
the mercy of rulers. No bony saint grilled
his eyeballs in the sun: the minister had
plenty to eat, was blessed with a wife, children,
and various servants. His bungalow stood
like a governor's mansion overlooking
garden and tennis court. He alarmed the dust
of villages in a Chevrolet that breathed
steam from its radiator; fisher of men,
hauled in shining netfuls of the converted.

Bred into this too easy ascendancy,
ignorant of our motives beyond wanting
to poison the brown boys in the orphanage,
my brother and I squeezed the juice from flowers
into the stream that brought them drinking-water.
And once, with a cruelty I could neither
recognise nor have explained, I flung a stone

when one of them dared to enter the compound,
and started the blood flowing above his eye.
Concealed in the musty dark of a cellar,
I heard my father's just and dangerous voice
as he opened the door and peered too briefly
to catch me cowering among the piled planks.

WALKING WITH MATRON

In the Nilgiris, a platoon of Christ's cadets
with uniform shirts and topee helmets, we were
marched under tropical leaves by Matron, singing
'Stand up, stand up for Jesus'. She led us firmly
out of the hooting shadows to revelations
of sky and mountain, precipices with slow white
ropes of water dropping three thousand feet to the
empty plain, and we rested there in the silence
that calmed her voice as she told us about the one
sheep that was lost and found. We filled our handkerchiefs
with tea berries, put beetles like gems in boxes
velveted with moss. On the way back I managed
not to crunch my peppermint: it dissolved on my
tongue like a sliver of ice, and my bitten mouth
was cool and peaceful. But near the school we halted,
while Matron lifted her walking-stick and battered
a small brown snake to death, her spectacles glowing.

DAVE MORGAN

I recall how Dave Morgan, blocky and tough,
a compact monster, would bare his teeth like fangs
as he flattened his victims against a wall
and pressed with his strangler's thumbs. Matron revised
his tongue with carbolic soap when the devil
put filthy words in his mouth. One afternoon
he raised a buzz of rumour by taking off
into the hills, at sundown was recaptured
in the tea plantations.—I often wonder
how he made out, and on which side of the law;
whether he drifted in desperation, trapped
by a hopeless temperament, or, steely
behind a desk, with dictaphone and wall chart,
learned to endure the hot wind, the thorns rooted
in boyhood, converting madness into power.

THE ENTERTAINERS

Our native servants—Adam, Benny, Joseph—
like bachelor uncles jovially indulged
my brother and me, carving neat replicas
of knives and guns, or making brushes we dipped
in wet mud to adorn the rustic fences.
They would chase us round and round the bungalow
till we were drunk with laughter, or from slips
of fir weave fragrant temples for teddybears
to squat in like golden idols. One morning
they taught us names for the small white penises
displayed at their request, but didn't show us
their big brown ones. Instead they performed again
the fire trick—lifted brands from the kitchen stove
and stood there smiling, gripping them in their fists.

HOLIDAY IN LIMERICK

Home from an Ulster boarding school
I dreamed away the hours in my father's church—
cosy, uninformed, one of the Methodists
too few and peaceful not to be tolerated,
too poor to instal an organ. I composed
my mood all morning on a grand,
bathing in lustrous ninths entitled 'Lotus'.

Cycling home, I loved to push hard
into the wind that made the Shannon glint;
to see, in floods of air above the castle,
rooks straining too and lapsing,
and in the far stillness, where God began,
the curve of Keeper Hill.

All form, picture, visible music!
Even if those ladies with Oxford gowns
had mentioned Sarsfield and the Wild Geese,
that would have been mere history, far away
in the small end of a telescope.

THE DANCERS

These more aesthetic forms of experience must be carefully distinguished from those which indubitably involve a change of one's nature.

—Carl Jung

1

First light, faint and cool,
graces the sleeping village.
At low tide, alone,
I watch the gulls
bathe with a slap of wings
in the freshet sliding
into the salt shallows of the harbour.

How long since the missionaries brought
holy baptism here to sweeten
the bitter soul? Today the unbelievers
come for holiday healing: cars
glut the small streets that wind
uphill to where the Wesleyan chapel stands.

The place is deserted now
except for the splashing gulls
and me, with the taint
of fear and lassitude in my blood,
thinking of this and of things
the Methodist preachers blazed
for good or ill: how often did belief
in the need for grace and cleansing
make bitter the sweet soul?

In a cottage parlour where
I crossed out words and phrases
hangs a sampler stitched
a hundred years ago by a teenage girl:
two evangelical stanzas, then
'The serpent beguilèd me and I did eat'.
Remembering now, I drop this irony into
a chaos that the mind,
intent on wholeness, naturally—
shaping some argument about
my craft, my father's mission, and the Word—
has started to inform.

2

On the island rock standing
offshore like a crust of jet
in foils of running silver,
St. Clement lived—whether
scared into uneasy quietude,
scouring his soul with the rough wind
for his redemption only, or becoming
a radiant centre to relay the Word,
who knows? Some believe in
holy emanations, as though a grace
could flow from his praying spirit
into the light and air
and the sea's voice, to stream across
the harbour and through the village,
seasoning with a subtle immanence
the grain of human life.

But Gautama returned to make
words out of the Word, obscure codings
for luminous apprehensions;
Francis danced his joy
before the cardinals, preached
love to citizens and to sparrows;
and Wesley, who had written once
'a quarter before nine I felt my heart
strangely warmed', went out on horseback
to win the mining towns.
Eighty years after, Billy Bray of Truro,
husband and profligate, who prayed
in desperation through
a six-day hell, knew
the moment his life changed, and brought
his tidings gladly to the market place.

3

In Cornwall, dreaming men
could stride into sweet nests
of fern and heather, whispering hollows,
and drop two thousand feet
through a howling blackness.
Peering in, we lobbed
a ball of rock, and waited.
Three times we heard it thud,
the note changing, diminishing, until
its plumb fall into pinpoint depth

stunned from the earth's drum
in a far-off echoing dark
the last word: *doom.*

Their faces deathly under candle flames,
fingers grappling rungs, boots tapping,
they journey down into
a trapped asphyxiating night,
to bear the pick's shock
at the level's end hour after hour,
hugged by the stale heat, the haze of filth
fastening on skin and lungs.

The will has grown
tough as the body, turned wretchedness to
enduring, till a man can love
the rich rock he curses, his dry spirit
pause for a draught of sympathy or praise.
But not Billy, the reprobate
who made them roar with laughter
a week ago: his lips,
famous for their speeding
of beer and blasphemous wit,
mutter remotely now, his stare
takes root in an inward vision.
The hardness he cracks open—
by turns listless, frenzied—
is more than the earth's bone,
his labour more
than the day's wage will token.

Fear of flood and rockfall,
of missed footings, the drop
to annihilation—this they had learned
to tolerate through the long sober stints,
to escape from in the dissolutions
of drunkenness and lust.
Hell was familiar, finite, tangible,
until the preachers came
transforming, amid tears and hallelujahs,
fact into symbol, known torments into
the unimaginable horrors of perdition.

Billy Bray, his will strung tight,
lives one rung at a time, drags upward
the dead weight of existence; sweating, feels
the tug of uncanny air,
and hears the pit breathe

Let go, fall, finish ...
but glancing up, and seeing
the blackness pricked with daylight,
prays, hardens his grip,
and climbs again in the soft candleshine
he wears upon his brow.

4

Alone on the sixth day, lost
in the nightstorm of his mind, he turns
to the first and simplest act, the firm
reality of touch: the Word,
cradled in miner's hands,
opening like bread broken, like split rock,
reveals the buried light of his salvation:
Ask, and it shall be given you;
seek, and ye shall find;
knock, and it shall be opened unto you.

Perfect in faith now, his prayer deep,
he moves from sorrow into the dancing
stillness of the Word beyond words,
and filled with amazing love, his spirit
clean and light, opens the cottage door
on a place he never lived in: 'I remember
this, that everything looked
new to me—the people,
the fields, the cattle, the trees. I was like
a man in a new world.'

Unearthly transformations—letting in,
deeper than all theologies,
the love that casts out fear!
Some say the will becomes
pure prism—or a jewel
hoarding a little daylight still
in obdurate particles, while the rest
is medium for epiphanies of colour.

Monstrous when the soul gorges on
the entire spectrum, and black opacity
declares itself translucent.
Better recluse then, or it will shape
the world with fire and rack,
needle and gas, proceeding like Der Führer
'with all the assurance of a somnambulist
where Providence dictates'.

These others tantalise, made whole by love
(the heart 'strangely warmed') yet so exacting
their disciplines could warp
lives that had trembled in the storms
of their great sermons. Wesley's rule
expelled 'disorderly walkers' from the classes:
and what was their desperate end—dropping
through fear's black shafts—
whom grace never shocked into the sober
euphoria of the saved.

And Billy Bray? About intolerance—
except to note a brief
offensive on the vanity of beards—
biography is silent. For the rest,
it seems he stopped drinking once and for all;
in meetings he would dance and shout
for pure joy; his wit was a bright knife
shredding the devil's arguments, his prayers
worked miracles of healing.

The truth was poorer, maybe.
Yet something happened: no legend
grows from history without
a living root to grow from.
Something was reached, released:
underground water
rising pure in the parched well—
love by its own pressure
casting out emptiness.

Logos, Atman, Tao ... words,
no longer needed when their definitions
fade in the sudden brilliance of their meaning.
'A poor spectacle,' said Billy Bray,
'to have only the telling part of the love of Christ:
it is the feeling part that makes us happy.'
Something happened. Suppose a man, seeking,
found his humanity, became
his Self so instantly
through a paroxysm of fearful longing
it seemed a miracle, but was
the shaft striking water that's always there.

5

May they rest in peace,
Clement and Billy Bray.

Athough I feel
the need they must have felt,
I am past expecting
wonderful changes now.
A fear like theirs
is storm in the night sky,
ours a cold fret
blearing the roads, reducing vision:
few are scared enough to become saints.
And should I find
some credible affirmation of the Word,
it won't be in their doctrines.

Go down into
the depths of history, through
the creeds and the persecutions:
Mahatma Gandhi, peacemaker,
dies from a gunshot on his way to prayers;
George Fox lies ill in the jailhouse;
undying candle, Latimer's body kindles;
Jesus bleeds on the crux of life and death.
Over and over, taking
the preacher's myth for fact,
men got the meaning wrong.
Yet all may have possessed it:
what clear-headed Anaxagoras,
jailed for impiety, tried to formulate,
the people, unsuspecting, found perhaps
in songs, dances, delicate bowls, buildings,
communities bound by justice and by love:
what we might witness here in the lineaments
of rock and water, harbour and winding street.

The rising sun gilds
hermit's isle and preacher's chapel;
glancing from waves, dazzles me where I stand
above the turning tide.
And air that breathed on water
fills my blood, bringing
to every informed cell
in the body's universe
a slow sustaining fire.

Such things are natural.
And here too, where thought and feeling
haunt the flesh (though strangely beyond space),
the elements dance, a subtle
agency weaves a logic.

I call this faith of a kind:
to see in art
the nature of the mind,
and to suppose it shapes
from chaos, from the absurd,
a structured wholeness that implies the Word.

ROCKS

'To go where they will'—
leaping the waterfall,
springing from rock to rock among
the pools, the sinewy glides—
means less, or nothing at all:

a game of win or lose
on tilted planes of granite,
whose strict alternatives compel
the mind to dance their pattern
and then to choose.

The man's decision marries
action to circumstance:
a future is woven from
the thread his quick stride
like a shuttle carries.

The boy follows, intent
and accurate—often as not
daring a new direction
though it were safer
the way his father went.

Silent, wary, locked
in their own freedom,
they hear the unending flow
sing irrepressibly while
it goes where it has to go.

PROGRESS OF THE LOGOS

Sharks prowl the paleozoic seas;
cancers bloom in the bones of dinosaurs;
hominids, by the light of reason, make
languages, gods, wars.

Strife keeps the world in tune, says Heraclitus;
Empedocles adds the counterflow of Love;
in Jordan the Word Incarnate bows his head
beneath the holy dove.

Eagles and doves divide the public will—
national pride locks with national shame:
the president calls a conference, and a child
burns in the napalm flame.

'Tension of opposites'? 'Christ at the world's heart'?
The mothers are still weeping. Let us pray
to our own deeps for wholeness: the Word will use
whatever comes its way.

THE SHAPE

He was the light rising
each day, the full circle.
His image grew from rain-seeds
dropped on pools, and shone
dark at the centre of the eye.

His work was seen
in the nine limpid shells
that kept the earth
safe as an embryo, making
incomparable music.

The electron's orbit
and the nucleus of the cell
conform. Even the stickleback's
ripening tumours
remember to look like globes.

WALLS: FOUR VARIATIONS

I

The walls insist. Whatever
their form, substance, durability,
not life nor death avoids them.

These a part of me, built and crumbled
in my own growing and lapsing,
or shaped by me somewhere along the way.

Others to welcome or oppose
my many arrivals: part of you,
or shaped by you somewhere along the way.

I flow, feeling the change
of stone, flesh, language
no more than a stream might feel the earth changing.

Two-faced, they attend us always—
part and protect, confine and keep us free—
making even the first and the last darkness.

II

Heart in his walls of bone,
bone in the sea-filled cave.
The shock of infinite air
whose limits he'll discover.
Touching begins to see,
and then the names come
for images and desires.
The mind's synclines fill
with sediments of faith
that harden, fault, buckle:
from fatherland he'll quarry
words for the great walls,
and then stones. One day
he'll dream for his comrades
a just, enclosing presence
as he waits in the bartizan
and peers, like a child,
at the racking dawn.

III

From alga to Zarathustra
she worked in a new style, intricate and ironic:

used walls with a filmy lining, then
that sensitive glaze alone, to define a plasm
nourished by all she loved of sea and light.

Her delicate separations made
community, eating, and at last
passion. Below the strongholds
where blood rose to exquisite steel and syntax,
wave after wave shatters on crumbling rock.

IV

The dream they gave a child—
globe within globe, himself
snug at the centre, and beyond
the last stars, God—
he smashed with a man's contempt. Ethereal dust
settled in sparkling drifts and faded.

He told himself 'Nothing can stop me now.'
And nothing did. Six-sided,
vaguer than air, exact as glass,
above, below, all round,
it stunned each move to freedom like a spell.

He beat on emptiness till he dropped
inert, drained of himself.
Curled then in the cyclone's eye,
he dreamed a light that melted
panes of nothingness to a warm tide
floating him, nudging him alive,
breathing 'I am, I will'.

After a dozen strides the fear came:
his fingers pressed on deadness.
Above, below, all round,
rectangles of glassy air
returned his voice more slowly than before.

What reaches then of time, of space?
How many dooms of breaking and renewal?
Pounding on sky-high walls he lost count,
his cry took years to echo:
'Be merciful, master of the Chinese boxes.
Let me be dreaming, lord: O wake me, wake me!'

POWER FAILURE

Just when our minds engage
he starts contracting—
becomes a square of light,
finally a white spark
diminishing to a pinpoint:
and now, whether dissolving
or (could it be?) receding
beyond our vision, leaves us
completely in the dark.

TRY YOUR STRENGTH

Alone, supine, each of us left in peace
with the lid down. Heaven and hell
in a nauseous equilibrium, unbearable.
So the will moves, the blood prepares for action.

No justice weighed these plates of rock.
Some people flip them open,
switching the sunlight on;
others have to heave with their whole strength
to gain a slow illumination;
a few press and press on the dead stone
until their souls ache—
purchase at best a brief flicker,
slump back into themselves, and stare
for hours in the numb dark,
longing to fall asleep and never wake.

BOY IN FISHING BOAT
from radio news

With no food or water, that Jamaican,
tormented by the hot glare
of the Caribbean as the boat drifted,
and almost in despair,
still cradled his father's head
long after the last breath was taken.
But seeing the man was dead,
whispered a prayer and lifted

the dry body across the gunnel
and lolled it overboard with a soft splash.
For weeks no sail or funnel
came in sight. Delirium turned the flash
of ripples and their small sound
to monstrous atmospherics in a maze
where he could neither wake nor sleep ...
So few words to report him found
alive after twenty days:
then silence, immeasurably deep.

LOFTHOUSE COLLIERY, 1973

Somebody yelled *Get out!* as the coal-face split,
and thousands of lethal tons began to pour
from the black fathoms of an abandoned pit.
The miners raced from its terrible breath and roar
through half a mile of darkness. Young Cotton ran
beyond danger, but in agony of mind,
praying with every stride that his old man,
'a bit buggered in the wind', plodding behind,
would live, yet knew there wasn't a hope in hell—
and what could *he* do by turning back, but make
two deaths instead of one ... His father fell
as the packed water slammed him: *For God's sake
run, boy, run!* was his last cry
before his lips were muffled; then he gave
his lonely mind to whatever it meant to die
buried already in a violent grave.

SPRING NIGHT
for Muriel

Out on Killiney Hill that night, you said
'Remember how we promised to come up here
when snow is lying under a full moon?'
And I made no reply—to hide my sadness,
thinking we might not satisfy that whim,
ever perhaps, at least for years to come,
since it was spring, and winter would see us parted.

Sitting on the Druid's Chair recalled
the last time we were there, a night of icy

wind and moonlight when the sea was churning
silver and the distant hills were clear;
how we belonged to them and they to us.
Now there was no brightness—only a vast
obscurity confusing sea and sky,
Dalkey Island and the lights of Bray
submerged and suffocating in the mist.

And there was no belonging now; no vivid
elemental statement to compel
refusal or assent, making decision
easy; but a dumb neutrality
that challenged us to give it character
and view our own minds large as a landscape.
To you it was tranquil. Sinister to me.

Lying under the pine tree, looking up
at the small stars and breathing the wood's sweetness,
we spoke hardly a word. I could not tell you
I was afraid of something out there
in the future, like that dark and bitter sea;
and how my love for you would have me lonely
until the fear was broken. I could say
'Be close to me next winter and every winter;
we'll come up here to watch the snow by moonlight'—
and that would be too easy. For I must give
to you whose meaning transcends moods and moments
nothing half-hearted or ambiguous,
but the perfected diamond of my will.

                                                        1952

HEARTWOOD: A SEQUENCE
in loving memory of Muriel (Nairn) Kell

I
IN EXTREMIS

Time and again, with astounded love and pity,
I think of the last moments—how she locked
with treacherous, twisting water, fought to the death
for the child made in her dark and gentle womb.
Did she know she had won, before the lethal coils
tightened around her, burying her alive
in a horror of baffled breath, till her lungs convulsed
and filled with the wrong element, and her mind's
appalled perception drowned in a race of dreams?

My love, my love, what was your passion then?
Though we lay in each other's arms, in each other's thoughts,
close as two people could be, how can I know
by imagining, how can phrases of mine tell,
the end of that violent coupling with the sea?
Was he god or devil, my invincible rival:
did you die in heaven, my darling, or in hell?

II
THE RESCUE

Gentle, warm, dark, the sea
you rocked her in; dreadful
the fire your love became
to give her breath. But once
wasn't enough, it seems:
what providence conceives
a crux like this?—the child
delivered into pain,
you strangling in warped floods,
the labour of your birth
into final stillness.

III
THE SCATTERING

Ashes ... What else?
A breath for new lovers
climbing Killiney Hill?
A clear harmonic in some timeless music?
Or, miraculously, your self
distilled from all you were, knowing for ever
'I', and even 'thou'? So many voices.
One, echo on echo, keeps saying
'Ashes, what else.'

IV
STARTING THE DAY

There's nothing left
where she performed the tasks
of anxious womanhood,
except a watch and comb,
a clothesbrush for stray hairs,
the big round mirror we chose
for checking masks.

V
WORKING LATE
The City of God, Bk XII, Ch 7

Silence is my self all round me.
Once it was good, because I knew
you were curled in the bed upstairs,
that I'd sleep to the rhythm of your
breathing, and we'd wake together
gladly, loving and undeceived,
allies against our sliding wills.
Now it is full of your absence,
the worst silence I've ever been—
charged with nothingness, implying
more than Augustine's dark logic.

But I know the other half still,
the tide rising: even the heart
of a silence mortal as this
can be redeemed: our children lie
sleeping upstairs, their lives my trust
renewed at each lonely waking.
Nothingness lapses too: a breath
of being fills the long small hours.

VI
FOR OUR GUESTS

Her going was dreadful; dreadful too the thought
I live with daily, that she's gone for ever.
Wishful, I can't accept it: love says no,
no, no, when reason says it's true—
and most of all when I am with the friends
I still think of as 'ours', for whom I smile
in honour of her courage. She was here
today, your gentle hostess, in the purpose
of children and of father to provide
once more the hospitality she offered.
If I have any faith or faithfulness,
it's in the kindness that I share with you:
when we break bread, listen, and talk, and touch,
move in the spaces where she drew her breath
and was the radiant centre of this home,
something I half believe seems wholly true.

VII
CHRISTMAS (A FRAGMENT)

Nothing can feel the same without you,
yet we have kept the appearances
unchanged, for survival and for love.
Christmas belongs to children, gluttons,
department stores, sentimentalists,
the remnant of the faithful. For some
it's another homely ritual
to celebrate affection, and now
one way of keeping you: we cherish
the customs you took part in. Is there
more our bleared vision won't let us see?
Belief starves in the long war between
hopes and arguments: since Christ faded
from Christmas, can I think you're with us
when we unwrap our gifts, or that we'll
ever meet again? There's only one
reason—of the heart—I listen to
intently: that the best love on earth,
the love of mother and child, is mocked
if death tears them apart for ever ...

VIII
DID YOU KNOW?

Did you know it was going to happen?
I remember your recurring
nightmare of violent water,
and how you went to hear
a lecture about bereavement:
no mention there, you remarked,
of the freedom of the bereaved.
I listened with no more
than a theoretical interest—
but oh, I'm haunted now,
my love, by the things you said,
and others you didn't think of.
The price paid for freedom
leaves a widower bankrupt;
and what can it mean, being free,
to a mind in sackcloth?

IX
REGRETS

The letter says 'You have
such good times to recall.'
Yes—but it's not like that:
across them shadows fall.
I think 'If death allowed us
to go back to the start,
I'd never say or do
anything less than kind.'
If it were possible
to reconstruct the mind,
to purify the heart,
that idyll might be true.

X
MISE EN SCÈNE

Three months after, leaving before long
the noisy solitude of a party,
I found the impulse I had waited for:
drove north on the empty roads,
walked for the first time
across the beach where she had drifted in,
and felt, without surprise,
nothing. A harmless-looking place
with a café and an Edwardian promenade.
But the waves did their best:
warping, they ripped from right to left
with a sinister hiss; and a circling beam
stabbed me over and over in the eye.

Smoking a cigarette in the parked car—
hand on the wheel, waiting,
numb in the uterine dark behind closed windows—
I heard out there, in here,
a continuous faint roar, like the sound of blood.

XI
NOVICE

Married bachelor, one year
I lived alone, sparely—
slotting coins in the meter,
having my rent-book signed.

Brown bread, salad, cheese;
reading till 2 a.m.;

beer at weekends; letters to her
and the kids: 'looking forward ... '

The ache of sleeping single after
eighteen years was nothing
compared with this. I know now
what I was practising for.

XII
RESISTANCE

Sometimes, hugged by a tense inertia,
I stare out of the window.
The glass gets dirtier every day,
fogs the apple trees, the poplars
swaying in quiet breaths of summer.

Too easily the haunted mind
drifts on warm wind,
turning it into spirit, never convinced
a loved person can be gone for ever.

Already tough green suckers feed
on rose-roots: remind me how, last August,
a hesitant stranger brought the first hint,
and how I stood, puzzled and apprehensive,
the clippers in my hand.

Blackness absorbs the veil of dirt,
the ruffled leaves, the sky.
In calm lamplight I wince with fear
as something raps the window—
but then remember: stressed in its steel frame
as rust builds up, a pane of glass is cracking.

I've watched with torpid fascination
its lines of least resistance, month by month,
cutting their crazy pattern. One of these days
it's going to bang like a pistol
and drop in clanging fragments.

No, I'm not falling for that.
One of these days
I'll have the glazier in,
swab glass with soapy water, cut back rank
romantic agonies with a pair of clippers.

XIII
TRIPTYCH

Think of the mind breathing
all that musty freshness
of myths, ideals, laws,
like a church filled with flowers;
and then, for the first time,
this treasured air becoming
the life of one who died:
a husband's conscience, vague
as sunlight through stained glass,
turned crystalline, the exact
lustre of her being.

Think of the flowers thrown
on a pile of garbage, rotting;
the church darkened, rain
streaming on spire and windows.
Myths of sinister night
hiss among leaves and gravestones
or whisper round the altar.
How can the mind believe
fragrance and light had meaning?
Where, ever again,
will someone lost be found?

Think of grey morning,
the journey into town,
a sooty church reflected
small in the wing mirror;
a widower with a conscience
guiding young readers through
lovely elaborations
of myth, ideal, law:
his heart's defences like
those labyrinths, his days
as curiously ordered.

XIV
MARRIAGE IS LIKE A TREE

After the flood, its roots are dying in air.
When twenty-two rings of tough growth
fell in a race of water,
the bark was lumpy with healed wounds,
the heartwood sound.

I recall, with a love that's inward now,
its many changes: foliage playing
in light, drooping in damp glooms
or stilled by rich calms of summer;
branches furred with snow, or their stormy thrashing.

How sad, these emptied places. But elsewhere
you find, again with sadness, trees that were hurt
too deeply, unnerved by pest and fungus,
hollowing to their last stand
against the rising wind.

It could be a kind of luck, being left
the ghost of a scarred tree
still healthy when it toppled:
leaves whispering through all the mind's seasons,
a root safe in the ground for ever.

XV
FOR THE YOUNG PEOPLE

My sons and daughters, what could I say to you
in a vast emptiness, that wouldn't sound
remote or insufficient or untrue
compared with the simple statement 'She was drowned'?
Yet, in an age when interstellar night
dissolves the Cross, the Ark, and Moses' rod,
I could still wonder whether it was right
not to have taught you to believe in God.

Finally, all I said was 'Try to be
as she'd have wished you—as you've always been.'
Sharing the work, concerned for one another,
learning to hope again, and helping me
to do the same, you span the void between
a mythic father and a real mother.

from **IN PRAISE OF WARMTH:**
NEW & SELECTED POEMS
(1987)

AT GLEN COE: 1976

A place for tourists now. In the parking bay
tyres crunch to a standstill. Cameras wink
at a piper massive as a monument,
cutting him down to size for snapshot albums.
But on the bridge below, by a dark pool
and a rowan tree, you hear the edgy sweetness
of chant and drone mix with the tangled notes
of water spilling endlessly on rock.
The rich primordial bourdon of the mind
begins its dreamy monotone: absorbed
in ancient stillnesses, you'd think the cries
and pistol shots echoed from icy crags
less than three hundred years ago meant nothing.
But mind grew into self, became aware
of selves, of kind and unkind, consonance
and dissonance—above the steady hum
no 'still, sad music', but the piercing skirl
of nerve and passion fined to artfulness.
I hear the folk tunes drifting down the glen
and can't forget the treacherous courtesy
that ended in a massacre. Kindest friend,
you know me now—hopeful when we're together,
loving the fells, the rivers, helping you
across the brimming stones; but every day
this radiant summer I've remembered death
and ways of dying—how natural kinship too
is torn by violence. While you gather cotton
from dried quagmire, I think of one whose children
swam with her in the sea she felt a part of
and saw the ungentle water stop her breath.

A FAITH IN MUSIC
The only appeal left is to mystery.
                    —John Hick

I search for the smallest clue—
no longer to find out
what suffering is all about,
but filled with the memory of you—
yet know it isn't worth the bother:
the intellect makes equal sense
of Chance and Providence:
one logic strikes against another.
But then, the chiming waves, the Word

so pure, so heart-cleaning,
that shock sends out!—its meaning
not understood but heard:
and how the mind lifts
clear of all premises, for once
floating on resonance
beyond the calculated shifts
of argument. My dear,
when I keep asking why
you of all people had to die
by violence, in pain and fear—
or, as some say, in a last glide of bliss—
every answer that comes to hand,
gleaming, out of rinsed sand,
is a mere hypothesis;
and were there time enough to look
I'd find each one, no doubt,
elaborately reasoned out
in a lucid, grave, no longer printed book.
But I'm content that no one knows,
for the unknown is where
making begins—unfathomed air
from which the world-breath flows:
and when I search for you,
my mind, still asking what is false and true,
but trying for love's sake not to care,
will let its eyes close
and see you, beyond rhyme and reason, there.

FRIDAY NIGHT
for Billy O'Sullivan, and in memory of Neans

At Morden Tower a vicar who likes Duns Scotus
reads his delicate poems. Out in the streets
helmeted bobbies are watching the well-oiled youngsters
whose roistering jeers alarm me. On the Metro
lunatic hairstyles, enticing thigh-length skirts,
glances and voices supercharged with beer
chafe the ambivalent loneliness of my ageing.
But then I think I'm wrong, that this is only—
though others who look the same will have been arrested—
'going gallant, girlgrace' in the current mode.
And yet their hopes are desperate: laughter lapses
quickly, as wit falters, into a blank
anxiety or sadness. Am I mistaken?—
for all the time I'm thinking of Neans and Billy,

lovely people, treasurers of the good,
the beautiful, the true, in a rotting world.
I remember Neans's laughter, her overflowing
gentle amusement at the fads and quirks
of cultured eccentricity, at the conforming
unconventionality of the rootless,
the lost romantics, gifted, exuberant, bubbling
with terrified self-assertion. But she spoke,
as you did, without contempt or condemnation,
secure in a loving order that house and garden
were visible tokens of. Husband and wife
clearly defined yet one—personal inscapes
instressed in a fine marriage: how you taught us,
Billy and Neans! And how we turn from the image
of helplessness, paralysis—handsome life
stilled at a stroke. But I listen to Duns Scotus,
I listen to Hopkins—though my undulant rhythm
be sprung from unbelief that longs to believe:
haecceity can't be lost: womangrace, mangrace,
kingfisher, stone, and bell, each is itself
for being more than itself—Christ, Logos, Instress
'playing in ten thousand places'. How shall Neans
or Muriel be unselved in the ground of selfhood?

This Friday night I rally a routed faith,
fashion a kind of prayer for you, dear Billy.
Nine years away from tragedy I am scarred,
but you are bleeding, bleeding: how well I know
the agony you are in, that you can't get out of—
'and wouldn't ask to', I think, but then remember
Let this cup ... Even the Word Incarnate!
What can I do but offer you these rhapsodic
unmodish lines from a heart no longer simple
but haunted by old affections. God be with you.

1984

DECORUM

Cupped against your ear,
the far-off voice bearing
sad news is never plaintive
but gentle, brave, austere.

Passing the message on,
you exchange with a far-off voice

familiar phrase for phrase
calm as an antiphon.

Nor will you ever know
how voices may have faltered
after the phone released them.
The dead would have it so.

DEATH'S REPLY

I am not proud, nor do I seek dominion;
I do not destroy, or even sting.
Fire stings, and the nettle, and the scorpion;
violence breeds in every natural thing.

Innocent killers, you thrive on flesh or fruit;
guilty, you wreck and murder. You, not I,
sprang from the same imperishable root
as the wild energies of earth and sky.

Of the soul's destiny I know nothing;
but it may be, some part of you will thirst
for my Lethean purity, my soothing
emptiness, when life has done its worst.

TO THE SKYLARK AGAIN

Why—even here,
feeling the grass
resilient underfoot,
as I cross the moor
that holds the city at mind's length,
and catch the wind's feathery
thunder in my ear,
its ocean-echo within
myself, and above all
begin to hear
those delicate runs with which
you affirm your own way in your own
solitude, their trickle of clear
water at the heart
of interminable dryness,
lacing the air

you hover in, so on small wings
you dance to your own music—
why do I feel fear?

If only you knew,
remote in your urban pastoral,
how celebrated you are—
'blithe spirit', 'pilgrim of the sky',
soul of a violin rhapsody
ascending from a green shire.
That flight is over now except
in the Eng Lit syllabus
and *This Week's Composer.* The atmosphere,
in both senses,
has changed somewhat on Tyneside,
and all the things you were
dissolve in the apprehension
that rights of property and sex
are what your songs declare.
Forgive us: we had hoped to believe
in heaven. Yet heaven perhaps
is to be unaware
of being, purely to be:
perhaps, after all, you sing for sheer
joy. But we, blithe body,
are neither whole nor simple:
we hope and we despair,
studying the selves we might have been,
the selves we may be,
the selves we only wear.

Distance absorbs
the molecules of music:
only the wind's voice, a far-
off thunder, the ocean
haunting the hollow shell,
is with me now, and a stir
of memory: once I heard
the whisper in mountain grass, felt
loneliness, or fear,
as though it were all around me.
When we're lost in a solitude
nearer home, it is there
too—in the company of friends
who are strangers, or alone
in searching stillness, sure
of nothing—but wholly inward then,
secreted emptiness, the geode's heart
that only breaking can lay bare.

Dark now: the lamps are lit.
I come from an inner shore
to this, man-made at the moor's edge—
plunge in the roar
of traffic, cross the unholy river
into the glare
of neon, the coloured night
where the sound of fear
can be shouted down; and whether
life's centre be core
or cavity, till the hour
the lark rises to fill
the silence with himself,
no one will be alone enough to care.

THE RESCUE TEAM

Courageous, doing what they can.
How will they understand a death
as far from dying as this?
I see, through the blue lens I'm in
fur haloes and frosted beards.
I imagine the scouring cold of wind,
stress-warps in careful minds,
edgy humane voices
as they discuss me.

Now their arms lift, the steel
swings, bites with a shock
that blows faintly into my flesh
like breath and radiation.
They have started
breaking me from a block of silence.
The stillness of no longer caring
begins to crack; I feel
the pain being born again.

TWO TREES
for L.M.

Widower now, uneasy in the stern,
trying to learn contentment as you row
across the liquid light,

I keep in memory how she took her turn
at the oars on the same lake—
and then how you and I
stood this morning on the shore,
amazed by naked roots
not intertwining merely, but grown together
into one organism,
yet oak and sycamore perfectly themselves.
These things were signs and mysteries once.
I think 'Two partners', then 'Two partnerships'—
and hold that sweet suggestion in my mind,
trying to hope, trying to learn belief
in a time without conviction.
You take your turn, the oars cutting deeply.
Light on the lifting blades breaks and falls.

THE CLOUD

Down here it rises to the tap, made safe
for human cells with a dash of deadly poison.
You turn it into suds, tea, plasma,
stir it to stodge with oatmeal or cement.
Along the street it's filthy in the gutter,
under the street a foul hygienic flux.
In lanes it's puddles, in some idle corner
a stasis gorged with trash, a scummy trance.
You climb above the town: on granite curves
it's glides, cascades, gurgling polyphony.
Higher still it's authorised, dam-controlled,
dispensed in measured quantities through pipes.
Labour towards the summit: you will see
small streams becoming smaller, multiplying—
then hear them only, trickles beneath the heather.
Now there is form for neither ear nor eye,
but green vagueness, sponginess, where a hand,
pressing, fills with the cold clean liquid.
On naked rock and scree you feel the air
sharpen; you scramble hotly, and at last,
reaching the harsh emptiness where mind
has built an image out of stony chaos,
you stand chilled, alien, wind-rebuffed,
lost in the wet oblivion of the cloud.
How can you belong where all you see
is vapour and broken rock, where you feel nothing
except a lonely awe at the edge of life?

This is no place to be when fire is shrouded.
Yet here, while the elemental round goes on,
begins the local gift, the descent of water.
Someone down there is offering wine, or tea.

IN PRAISE OF WARMTH

I

Right and left will not make middle,
but hot and cold make warm.

II

Identity of opposites? Out of this world!
Being finite, I'm content with the tug-of-war.

III

The right tension, a gentle warmth,
the flute sweetly in tune.

IV

In the torrid zone you want iced lager;
in the frigid, soup. Warmth in both cases.

V

To enjoy the shower
you tune extremes with a subtle expertise.

VI

What grows from the waves of the Sahara,
the dunes of the Arctic Ocean?

VII

Filled with liquid air
the kettle boils even on solid water.

VIII

In liquid air a finger will turn to stone,
a microbe lie snug till its reawakening.

IX

Occupier away, pipes frozen.
Voyagers living dead for the far future.

X

'The bitter change of fierce extremes': pure hell
for 'soft ethereal warmth'.

XI

On cool nights we're warm in each other's arms;
on hot we roll apart to our sweaty broodings.

XII

A warm glow. 'Oh, how I love the fire!'
Embrace it then, my love, and report back.

XIII

'Lukewarm I spew thee out of my mouth.' Dear John,
how warm is warm enough without scalding?

XIV

The zealot's rage burns
like a meteorite with heart of ice.

XV

A lobster likes water, but not this.
The gourmet watches while the bubbles dance.

XVI

When they throw the switch and the lights wince,
a man's blood boils.

XVII

Panel, thumb, fireball—
or ice advancing to engross the warheads.

THE EXCHANGE

In 'Rock of Ages' or 'When I survey',
Louie the Loner's resounding baritone goes
zooming over pews, recalling for Bristol,
whose traders harrowed his forebears in their ships,
the only hope of the cotton pickers. Children,
with giggling affection, whisper 'Poor Old Joe',
remember the dark gleam of his wife, who played
the hymns for Sunday School till her last illness.
He loves the tall smooth pipes, and even more
their spread of sounds, from lyrical trebles to
the deep security of the pedal notes.
Each week he puts a pound coin in the plate
towards upkeep and salvation.

After the benediction, the smiles and handshakes,
he's off to the Old Duke, the beat of jazz,
his pint in a crowded corner—
every Sunday the soothing din, the sprawl
of yellowing posters on the ceiling,
grimy trombones and saxes hung like trophies.
He smiles hallo, says little. Deep inside him
the music presses warmly; beyond the door
it throbs towards the quayside, thins
like history over masts and water.
When the collection for the band comes round,
Louie, blissfully humming,
drops into the bag his clinking tribute.

TIME TRAVEL

We sat across from each other on the Metro.
She wouldn't have thanked me for my pitying rage
against the quantum vagaries that had made her
so touchingly unbeautiful. I wondered
whether she'd found the one young man in a million
gifted to love her face or overlook it.
At the next stop a woman twice as plump,
three times as old, sat down beside her. Neither
heeded the other, saw what my glance discovered
against all expectation: so strong a likeness
that here was the younger after forty years.
Eyes, nose, mouth, unchanged except by age,
induced again, without authority from

the lady who had learned to live with them,
a current of tender fury. Well, perhaps
both were indifferent to the promised land
of sex and marriage; if not, I could only hope
that one was going to town to meet her boyfriend,
the other wearing his rings inside her glove.

THE CHOOSER

Half-truths, clear and simple:
there's one, gift of the mountain,
sweet enough to drink;
another, far from land,
no thirst can bear.
The whole truth of the estuary
is subtly both yet neither.

The both-and man's perplexed,
finding he wants all three
and more—much more.
He has heard of a strange thing
in some place off the map:
salt and fresh made one
yet each purely itself.
He shrugs, knowing the tall tales
bred in the *Crown & Anchor*.

Meanwhile, searching a world
equally enigmatic,
he tries a new approach:
a whole truth on the mountain,
another far from land;
at the river's end, oddly,
the half-truth they add up to,
whose brackish two-in-one he needs
but hopes never to swallow.

There logic rests, until
the either-or man jeers
'Both-And or Either-Or!'—
then, seeing his comrade puzzled,
'Both-And *and* Either-Or?'.
The both-and man reflects, mutters
'Hell's·teeth', and starts again.

CRITICAL BOOKS

Squiggles and underlinings, queries, cries
of affirmation, ridicule, or rage,
brash tokens of a common enterprise,
welcome his late arrival at the page.
And when the text is clean, the margin clear,
it's hard to be content with drawing a map,
denying the impulse of the pioneer
to mark his trail with *Hm, Spot on,* or *Crap.*

Keeping his pencil caged—though what he's reading,
the very latest probe on *Lycidas,*
moves him to sympathy for Milton's ghost—
he prays, with a dark sense of mutants breeding,
to be retired before some gifted ass
prefixes 'deconstructionist' with 'post'.

THE FIRST CIRCLE

We could change to lenten eating,
read in the dead of night
without the central heating
in chairs hard and upright;
cut out smoking, keep
our aims above the belt,
and be disturbed in our sleep
by what Volodin felt.

That for a start. But flush
with bourgeois freedom, fetching
another pint, I lounge on crimson plush,
read till my head grows warm;
then, curled around my guilt, start sketching
a poem in almost academic form.

THE BUTTERFLY HEARS TCHAIKOVSKY

Did it blunder in from the street?
Worse, imagine it reborn
among the platform flowers,
the first venture of delicate wings
wafting it straight to hell.

Our minds flooded with metaphor—
Francesca, Paolo, the manic winds
they're whirled in, all music
out of a soul in torment—
we watch that silky flier
lost in the glare, bewildered by
the shock of storming brass.
Flickering, it soars, dips,
traverses, its frail career
scribbled on art in a real
violence. When the applause breaks
it's gone—twitching perhaps
beside a player's foot, finished off
by the tuba's final blast,
the sumptuous crash of gong and cymbals.

HYGIENE

Out of the staid familiar pile there slips
amazingly, like a cry of liberation,
a magazine called *Fitness*, with a piece
on 'Sensual Massage, the New Foreplay'.
I note, more patiently than usual, that
appointments are running late, and settle down
to learning from simple text and illustration
the five basic strokes and the choice of oils.
Two minutes for revision, then I'm called
to the delicate expertise of Miss Maloney.

I'm tilted back, obedient, relaxed, trusting—
off-duty archon subject to his slave.
No, please, not that!—let perilous fantasies
be rigorously suppressed. But oh, how sweetly,
how nearly, like the lover on Keats's urn,
she hovers at my mouth! I allow only
marginal vision of her glowing eyes,
her lips' tormenting ripeness, as she probes
and rasps and flicks with dainty discipline.

'Rinse please'—then it's over. I doff the bib,
put on my jacket, wish her a nice weekend,
and go with dignity. Now I step down stairs,
my tongue relishing surfaces and crannies
restored to freshness by a small quick pick.
I sign at Reception, leave by an arched portal,
and drink the air like a reader of *Country Life*.

THE SLAVE

Cheers, fanfares, the drums' thud,
    the soldiers' obscene bawling
tear like a cyclone through the general's brain
    behind his mask of blood.

At the hushed centre, clear and deep,
    Hominem te memento
hums over and over, hums and melts,
    lulling his pride to sleep.

He rides relaxed, though star and palm
    glow on his tunic—fingers
gently supporting the inclined rod,
    eyes utterly calm—

yet thinking 'All this—the line
    of senators, lictors, priests,
the sacrificial oxen, the spoils and crowns,
    the captives—all mine.'

In the cavernous heart of all this
    he cowers alone, listening:
over and over *triumphus* swells and bursts,
    ebbs in a long hiss.

Sick with life-weariness, guilt, fear,
    acids of war and intrigue,
who needs a charm against the supreme madness
    droned into his ear?

Seized with a ritual-defiling
    rage, his glance fired
for once with more than wine, he leans and mutters,
    through teeth tightly smiling,

Tace, tace! Then hears regret—
    its mild exacting impulse
the one reminder that defeat can bear—
    breathing *Me paenitet.*

FAMINE

No human being did this.
Nor God, you say—and I agree:
but you are sure of God, not I.

How then do you explain
millions in torment for so long,
even the children slowly dying?

Karma?—in droves, like Belsen?
God's refusal to violate
his natural laws? I'd give you that—

but why the faulty circuit
of sky, earth, seed, and human cell,
a Chain of Being whose links fail?

A dash of randomness?
Perhaps. 'God doesn't dice', but how
could pure machinery change and grow?

Or was Augustine right?—
and Sartre! who found *le néant* here
au sein de l'être ... comme un ver,

our own lack defining
what simply is—dry root, bare sky—
as something less than it should be.

Anima Mundi? Then
that she-he-it is breathing hell,
and 'God' has done this after all.

A mystery if you like,
divine law, nothingness, nature, chance:
but do shut up about Providence.

SENTIMENTAL JOURNEY
for L.M.

On Sundays there is still time.
  Plodding with sticks and hoods
like pilgrims, seeking what remains
  of rural peace, we climb
through bristling fences into woods,
trespass devotedly on proud demesnes.

But only if the way we chose
      happens to bring us there
after the promises it made.
      We go where the dream goes,
asking, without ill will, to share
the loveliness of dingle and cascade.

One perfect afternoon distilled
      from winter and spring, we found
a lively runnel to lead the way.
      It splashed through heather, spilled
joyfully under a bridge—and drowned
in a drugged river tinted greenish-grey.

Spotting a sign, *No Trespassers*,
      we walked on all the same,
as every true romantic should.
      And then, from hushed acres
that breathed with new life, there came
a sound like nails being hammered into wood.

Strewn cartridge cases, bright as blood,
      explained it. A scattering
of soft grey feathers lay near by.
      From coppices in bud,
startled, their quick wings clattering,
the doves flew out into a deadly sky.

We wandered on until the last
      cold shining of the sun
made thorny haloes round the trees;
      turned homeward then, and passed—
devoid of wildlife, sour and dun—
still waters dying of a slow disease.

But shrugged off disappointment, having
      each other to be with;
talked about visionary books,
      tales of the spirit's striving,
the meaning of the journey myth,
and the mystique of staffs and shepherds' crooks.

Then clicked our seatbelts on, resumed
      comfy suburban postures,
agreed it had been a pleasant day,
      and, souls charged with the gloomed
benignity of green pastures,
rose to the furies of the motorway.

THE GENTLEMAN WHO SNEAKED IN

Women! Persons! *Please!* Allow me to speak
just for a moment ... Thank you ... What I wanted
to say was this. To begin with, I understand.
No, I mean it: I do understand, and even
sympathise. In fact I'd go so far
as to call myself, with your permission of course,
a feminist. But there are, if I may say so,
feminists and feminists. Most of you here,
judging by what I've heard, would like to treat
men as they've treated women. I'm not surprised.
Age after grisly age of patriarchal
pride, insensitivity, exploitation—
no wonder you are militant! But consider:
has anything of enduring value ever
been gained by retaliation? Think, my friends!
Why would you take for model the sex you scorn?
Doing as they did, how would you help the world?
Cry out in protest, not in revenge and malice.
Firmly resist, but only in the name
of co-operation, sharing, mutual care,
equality, gentleness, all the lovely ways
that you can teach us now. We want to learn,
believe me. We *need* to learn if the human race
is not to ... Thank you, ladies. Thanks for listening.
You're very kind ... Thank you. I wish you well.

THE ISLAND

Thirty fathoms, clear as the mind of Adam.
Working at the gunwale
I saw my dropped watch twinkling down
all the way to the clean sand.

They couldn't leave well alone—any more
than the rest of us since the year dot.

We had to keep our eyes covered.
The flash x-rayed our hands. My back
hurt in the fireball's breath.
We got the count ... two, one, zero,
then turned to face the light. It was unbelievable,
the cloud with its root of flame, the boiling colours.
The bang came, then a long crumbling roar.

The shockwave thumped us like a force-eleven
and half the lads went sprawling.

Those experts, know-alls, swore
the blasts were safe, given the altitude.
Wrong as usual. The black rain
poisoned us to the bone.
Plankton gorged on dirt, fish on plankton,
we on the fish. A lot have died of cancer.
One had a film of blood across his eyes.
Some had cataracts, skin disorders, even
kids born twisted.

Thousands of birds were blinded. Those that lived
were screaming, crashing into the trees and ships.

I'm rotting slowly towards a wheelchair.
I dream back to the slog and ache
that seem like paradise now,
the coral crust, the pure deep water.

PATHETIC FALLACIES
April 1986

Reagan: 'a surgical attack
on terrorist-associated targets'.
The surgeon's hand was shaky.
BBC mikes in Tripoli gave us
the voices of bombed civilians
telling of loved ones killed or maimed.

We heard later how climates are being changed
by man's dirt in the air.
Spring hasn't come, the sowing hasn't been done.
Instead of sunshine and April showers,
week after week of cold wet wind.
All day the rain has been pouring down
while the news has been pouring in.

It's political licence now. The poet's kind
was venial by comparison—and to plead it
would hardly be called for if he wrote today
the ravaged world is weeping.

REMEMBERING LIMERICK

For me, taught in an Ulster school, the South
meant holidays, dreamy solitude, whispering roads—
history the Magna Carta or the Armada.
From the bridge across the Shannon I gazed with love
at a glint of water, then trees, castle, a sky
spattered with rooks. Beyond, when my mind was clean,
the enchantment of the hills began—and all
was bathed in music. The peals from any church
were flash-floods to brim the heart. In our neat manse
there was no talk of policy or dogma:
goodwill and the universal were our commitments.
One evening, when I passed through broken streets,
waves that should have stirred in me like a cry
came weak and fitful, as from foreign stations.

Now, after many years on the other island,
I'm no more Irish or English than before—
only aware, with a sad self-inclusion,
of how things were, and are, and will continue
till one slow age of feeling dies to another.
Hearing the news from Bogside or the Falls,
and having read, long out of the classroom,
something of Sarsfield and the Wild Geese,
I sip sour blends of distance and compassion.

ROCK AND WATER
(1993)

ADVICE FROM A STRANGE VISITOR

No, it's too late for this.
Why the invisible lines that a bloody fight
and a signature can change, compounding
the nonsense of those map-locked colours?
And what are the native soils you sing of?—
soils that belong to all or none,
found the world over.
Was there some good in the primal jealousies,
that you parade banners and guns long after
the merging of your tribes?
Maybe you fear your real colours
will all give way to one, your styles be lost,
the entire species dance to the same music.
But what could frontiers do to prevent that?
They can't keep out the sound waves, video waves,
languages, paintings, instruments, fabrics, foods,
passions that need no visas. Well, why should they?
These things are not reductive.
Mixing their local essences with your own,
you serve the many-in-one, the one-in-many.
Communications variegate the world;
their energies flit through the comical-tragic walls
dreamed up by statesmen—a swift electric wind
like the substance of all things, whispering
'People, become yourselves, dissolve your nations.
It is too late for this.'

CUTTY SARK RACE, 1986
for Jeanne Harvey

Eighty names under eleven flags,
the tall ships are preparing.
Consensus of the skippers will decide
the winner of the trophy—
not for coming first, but for doing most
to promote friendship among the nations.
No walls, no warheads. Germany, Poland, Russia,
Britain, Ireland, Italy share the wharves
down-river from Tyne Bridge.
Its great bow spans the water like a sign.

Yesterday we joined the people strolling
among the snackbar smells and the funfair's clamour,

to gaze at booms and rigging, the strakes' long curves
lifting to perfect union at the bows.
Sailors aboard and citizens on the quay
decoded syllables, smiles, gesticulations
to touch each other's lives. When night fell,
the air was salt with jazz and roistering shanties,
then subtler compounds festively exploded
and glittering sprays of colour drenched the sky.

Now we are two among the early thousands
gathered on Tynemouth grass.
With monumental pride, above the guns
that thundered at Trafalgar,
Collingwood stares across the estuary
where no one stopped the Danes.
But friends and families peer up-river,
watching for shapes that will recall
the trade routes, cargoes of tea or wool,
stress and courage the same in all races.

We wait for hours, then masts as fine as needles
appear at the last bend.
Applause crackles like flame along the crowd
as yawl, brig, schooner and barquentine
grow to their full splendour and glide past,
all afternoon lighting the people's eyes,
winning their love and their understanding.
We raise binoculars, pick out names and flags.
Ships from eleven countries
remind us what we deeply care about.

Someone says 'Look, she was nesting here.'
We weren't prepared for this, a small brown bird
—some grass dweller, lark or pipit maybe—
fluttering back and forth over the crowd,
holding a scrap in her beak, plaintively crying.
Yes, we care—her kindred, makers of homes,
packed like aliens on her territory.
But what can be done? We watch her, equally helpless,
in pity sharing her torment, filled with anger
at randomness and irony even here.

There's fallout in our minds; but eighty ships
now line abreast beyond the harbour
have something more to say, and we're attending.
Brief celebrants, we watch our purest hope
declared in full sail on the open sea.
Kruzenshtern, Dar Mlodziezy, Falken, Outlaw,

Kaliakra, Eendracht, Asgard, Malcolm Miller,
far from the presidents and the armies,
are slowly melting into light and rain
under a spectral arc.

AN AFRICAN BOY
for Paul Lomongin, enquiringly

When Karamojan warriors
resisted government troops,
victims of the crossfire
fled from shattered homes
to the bleakness of the hills.

Children were missing later;
many had lost their lives.
But you, nine years of age,
'favourite subject maths,
hoping to be a teacher',
smiled into the lens.

Letters weren't allowed.
You sent a pencil drawing—
huts and a single tree;
I a Christmas card—
sheep in a winter sunset,
a note explaining snow.

Then the policy changed:
no sponsoring in future.
Although they'd use the cheques,
I couldn't help recalling
a film about a river
slowing to a marshy end
somewhere in the savannah.

But now I'd rather think
of water gliding deeply
into a dazzling sea.
Dear Paul, I hope a friend
working in Karamoja
will help you dream that picture
and ask you what it means.

THE MOORINGS

These boats of different kinds,
of several shapes and colours,
the shabby and the sleek,
the old and new, all
point one way in the tide.
And listen—cables tapping
masts in the warm wind
are making gamelan music.

Nice, you'd say; but people
are flesh, not fibreglass,
and parables aren't plans.

DELIVERING LEAFLETS

There are eager ones, gulpers
of all you have to give,
types with tough moustaches
that taunt it like a sieve,
and some whose grudging grin
demands you fold it small
before they'll let it in.
Several bark, and are known
to enjoy as well as paper
a tasty knucklebone.
When your hand dares to invade
the hollow hell between
two snappy plates of steel
edged like a butcher's blade,
you're in luck if it doesn't fall
with your gift and a rich cascade
of blood into the hall.
Sensible ones have a single
valve to admit the word
and stop the wind. But alas,
an envelope full of turd
or of poison-penmanship
is never excludable.
I, with something more
overtly political
to take from door to door,
am trying to beat the boredom
by seeing various kinds
of letter slots as minds.

REMEMBERING PAINE

Good for you, Tom, 'drinking copiously
of brandy in the tavern,
mixing with none but the lower orders'—
scorned by the higher, including
Washington. Once your words
kindled his army; now you are
'a troublesome Republican, dangerous to
religious and moral rights'.

I hope, had I been in the New World
the week you died, I would have mourned
beside your lonely grave—
wishing you, outcast and 'atheist',
your true deserts from the one god
they couldn't understand.

CONVERSATION IN A CITY PUB

Him, quiet in a corner: 'What are you writing?'
Me: 'Just a memo'—sort of. Later he clicks
a flame before I can strike my match; declines
(too mild) the brand I offer by way of thanks.
I write some more. Fretful, he casts again
on the dark water—'You are so entertaining!'—
and now my attention's hooked.
                        He's young, lean-faced,
with hay-blond hair, blue eyes that are growing tired
from the drinks he's had, and a slow articulation
I take to be North Germanic. Yes: he sailed
three months ago from a Swedish port to Whitby.
'Nice town,' I remark. 'You had some business there?'
'No business. That is the place the boat was going.'
'I see.' But he knows I don't. 'I came,' he tells me,
'to make a mental holiday—to escape.
Sometimes you too escape?' 'I suppose I do.'
'And where do you go?' 'Well, here—or another pub.'
'I understand. But what is the thing from which
you try to escape?' 'Myself.' He likes the answer,
reaches out for a cigarette (a strong one),
and triggers the flame again.
                        'How about you?'
I ask him. 'What are you taking a holiday from?'
'You might say killing.' 'Killing? Are you a soldier?'

'A soldier, yes, but not of the normal kind.
A mercenary—you know?' He searches me.
'A mercenary: I find that rather frightening.'
'No, you must not be frightened. Do I appear
a frightful person?' I leave the question floating.
'Where did you work?' 'South Africa. Paraguay.
Various places.' 'Who were you fighting for?'
'I fought for the state.' 'Against the freedom movements?—
the blacks, the peasants? Did you despise the people?'
'No, I shall please explain: I was never against
the people.' 'And yet you killed them?' 'Only a few.'
'A few or a thousand, what do the numbers matter?
You killed them without a motive.' 'A man must live.
That is a motive, yes?'
                          I excuse myself
and make a trip to the loo, where a strident voice
is saying 'You're reet, m'n! It's the same fuckin story
every time y' gan t' the fuckin garage!'
Back in the bar, I try to make some sense
of the deeper story. A quietly-spoken Swede
is straining against oblivion, holding apart
the sliding doors of order, safety, silence.
A mental holiday? No. Confused and fearful,
he mentions enemies, dark self-inquisition,
options to worry over. He could return
to a country where he saved the President's life—
but that would mean more killing, and now he feels ...

So much for the entertainment: he longed instead
for a priestlike hearing. Or so it seems until
he slips into Christian names, and where do I live
and what do I do. I tell him, glance at my watch,
pretend with guilty relief that I have to go.
He smiles and offers his hand. Its grip is gentle.

DOCUMENTARY FILM (SRI LANKA)

My father had to learn
Tamil and Kanarese.
He spoke them like a native
among his mild converts.

Tonight I see farmfolk
drilling in battledress,

even boys and women
learning to handle guns.

'Free from all weaknesses'
the record goes: no sex
or alcohol or gambling,
a pure devotion now.

Firm bodies, glowing eyes,
rifles carried proudly.
Instead of necklace charms
ampoules of cyanide.

Then tearful smiles, portraits
to honour the Black Tigers—
suicide martyrs, drivers
of trucks like massive bombs.

Outnumbered but still deadly:
guerrilla tactics, nerve.
The leader godlike, hearts
filled with adoring faith.

Differing speech and cults,
Colombo versus Jaffna,
the world's oldest story
retold with new names.

Grievances unredressed
cry out for heroism:
the strong take notice when
the weak become strong.

As homes blaze and bodies
give their blood, somewhere
minds calmly absorb
the Gospel or the Veda.

ROOTS

Political verse? Promote it if you must—
but why not ethical? Strains of envy, spite,
injustice, avarice, pride, deceit, mistrust
warp any institution, left or right.

I too abhor the purges, the repression,
the slavery that keeps the bosses fat;
spying, imprisonment, torture, forced confession,
the insane pretensions of the autocrat.

Hearing you put the case for revolution
if protest comes to nothing, I agree—
but fear the people's will in execution,
the harsh euphoria of the newly free.

What will your slogans matter when internal
fires have made opposed commitments fuse?
The labourer kills as blindly as the colonel,
told he has nothing but his chains to lose.

After the coup, politics as the art
of government will shatter a single dream
to a score of aims, the brotherhood fall apart,
leaders wrangle till one becomes supreme.

Democracy, freedom, equality, jobs for all!
At first they mean it—hope at least to find
decent approximations; then they stall,
weaving grim agencies to hide behind.

Used soundly or corruptly, power remains.
What if the workers make it theirs at last?
Will there be no dark souls or cunning brains,
no dubious motives when the votes are cast?

Suppose the many are played on by the few,
the people's say-so won't continue long.
Rank schemes will flourish as they always do,
spelling not right and left but right and wrong.

End class and privilege? Even if you can,
that's surface work: will levelling put a stop
to tangled growth, make a new kind of man?
I'll call you radical when you raise a crop!

SECULARISM

This fear I feel
is perhaps a whisper
of what the heretics felt
when they were called for trial.

The power is passing
to your elect, its greed
for establishment
as huge as ever.

Be numbered always among
the clear, the kindly—
and join us, when you too
are marked, in the high retreats.

THE VICTIMS

1

 Chuang, would you say the same
if you were with us now? At a deep level
nothing has altered much
since the time of the Warring States,
when bureaucracy grew and the schools offered
rival theories of government.
Deeper still is the Never-Changing:
we have your thoughts on that.
But did you ever imagine
the redhot pincers, the black
gleam in the eyes of experts,
cries threading the corridors?

 You praise Wang T'ai of the chopped foot.
In Lu his retrospective wisdom
brought him as many disciples as Confucius.
His 'wordless teaching' was
the oneness of the myriad things,
the perpetual flow of *ch'i* and its transformations.
Losing a foot was like shaking off mud.

 But when it happened?—the ignominy,
the closeness of cruel hands and voices,
the terror under the blade?
Of these, Chuang, you say nothing.

2

 Now they apply electric currents
to genitals, ears, lips,
burn eyeballs and nipples with cigarettes,

the skin with flame or acid;
beat the soles of the feet, break bones,
gouge out eyes, extract with pliers
fingernails, toenails, hair.

Women are violated as well as men,
children as well as adults.
Listen: 'My crime was to shout
Allahu akbar: God is greater.
Four days I was tortured with electricity.'
He was thirteen. Another,
blue from the currents, nails pulled out,
blinded with caustic drops,
begged the informant 'Please look after
my parents. I am their only son,
they have no one else in the world.'
And this: 'I am disabled with
paralysis of the leg.
They beat me till the calliper-rod was broken.'

Regretful words graced
the wall of a smashed clinic:
'Dear Kuwaiti doctors, we are sorry
but we are under orders.'

3

Is it true that in your culture
pain was nothing compared with being deformed?
For us, torments of body and mind,
above all what the innocent bear
at the hands of the proud and cruel,
make many despair of God—
our teasing version of what you called,
with a clear discrimination of fact and symbol,
the Ancestor of the myriad things.

Who or what might have made
a stillness deep down
for mother and father, girl and boy
hurt by the rod, the fire, the phallus?
Allah? The thought of Allah? Maybe.
But, as you held that all things, dark and light,
spring from the never-changing One,
for these they are all the will of Allah.
'He misleads or guides whom he pleases'—
and the misled must burn in hell.
For a moment, Chuang, indulge

our tender reasoning. When the dark and light
are hate and love, who can explain
the torturer to the tortured?
What comfort for the outraged heart
if God empowers the outrage?

4

Many—among them Herbert,
a faithful priest and a fine poet—
have searched for understanding. You and he
came close, I think, on at least
the oneness and the flow. Listen again:

These are thy wonders, Lord of power,
Killing and quickning, bringing down to hell
*   And up to heaven in an houre;*
Making a chiming of a passing-bell.
*   We say amisse,*
*   This or that is:*
Thy word is all, if we could spell ...

These are thy wonders, Lord of love,
To make us see we are but flowers that glide ...

Here's Hopkins, a priest also,
praising a nun on a storm-lashed ship.
(Like Herbert, though, he'd hardly have let
your Way and his Word be twinned.)

*   Ah! there was a heart right!*
*   There was single eye!*
Read the unshapeable shock night
*   And knew the who and the why;*
Wording it how but by him that present and past,
Heaven and earth are word of, worded by ...

Heartfelt wording too from the poet-preachers.
May neither they nor the drowned nun,
nor you, Master, nor I,
have been the dupes of a metaphysical dream—
though in the end their teaching yearns
from yours like branch from trunk, to tell
of power secreting love.

5

Execution silenced
a Palestinian called Jesus,
preacher of love and loving healer,
whose sayings, recorded in our Bible
and in papyrus books by so-called
heretics, sound at times
a bit like yours. Thomas, for instance, gives
'The kingdom is within you and without';
'I am the All: if you split a log
or lift a stone, there you will find me.'

What if the cross had been
for torture only, and that wise
mysterious Jew had spoken
after his crucifixion?
Might he have told, as you did,
the power without the love,
or, love being lost, denied even
the wholeness, the single flood
of energy, spirit, *ch'i*, and so
the unfathomed kinship of the many?

All we know, supposing
our Matthew and Mark were right,
is that a great shadow covered the land
before the victim, wrists and feet
nailed to the wood, stopped breathing,
and at the last moment
his anguish cried in the words of an old poem,
'My God, my God, why hast thou forsaken me?'

Not even a whisper for the dying in pain?
Your teaching draws me, but still I'm sad
that there may have been no First Person
to care what the caring Nazarene felt
and the millions desolate through the ages;
at best what a gifted scholar
calls without irony, Chuang, the Tao at play.

LEVELS

Yes, it is all, in its many appearances, water—
all one and wonderful, from the sand's glazing
to the mountain-drowning darknesses of the deep.
But tell me, who wouldn't rather swim than paddle?
And who, loving to range beneath the surface,
expert with mask and flippers, wouldn't assume
the bathyscaph's downward-soaring power, to glide
in clear black space towards galactic shoals?

ROCK AND WATER

Here is the rock, a mighty V
whose tops are sometimes sharp against the blue,
sometimes obscured by mist;
and here the water, flowing
in lovely cataracts and glides.
Being tall and hard, the rock believes it's nobler.
The water says nothing, but keeps on singing
and softly, smoothly, endlessly caressing,
and moment by immeasurable moment
making the V deeper.

I see the shiny inklings on high crags
when rain comes, their forms determined
by granite gnarls and grooves.
I see the flood-wrapped boulders far below,
where every slide and swell and swirl,
every cascade and pool,
is made in perfect intimacy
with hump or jag or crevice.
What is the stream but water shaped by rock,
the gorge but rock being slowly shaped by water?

'This is wisdom,' I heard the sage declare.
'Both rock and water are the way,
fitted as light and shade, as high and low.'
Glad to be wise, and hoping to be wiser,
again I sat at his venerable feet.
'Seek the low ground: follow the way of water.
This is wisdom,' he said. One morning, perhaps,
I shall return and say, lowly as water,
'Master, behold this troubled pool
where wisdom and confusion dwell together.'

THE WAYS OF WATER

A pond where
bubbles rise,

a flashflood's
ebullience,

a cascade
and a pool.

DEEP IN THE HILLS

Deep in the hills we came across some odd
philosophers who still unravel 'God'.
One of them tried (in vain!) to make us see
the word means 'Emptiness and You and Me'.
Another said, pooh-poohing the concept *I*,
'Because you don't exist you cannot die.'

ROCCO

At feuist I considered Rocco
d'gradest guy in d'weuild.
He useta drive d'broads crazy—
gliddery eyes an' hard slim body,
sheuits fit fer a dook. But y'know
what made 'im tops? I'll tell yuh.
Rocco was fyer all through
an' ice all through, if y'get me.
Quick an' shooer, brain like a di'mond,
never scared. An' jeez, could 'e spread d'lead!
After 'is kid brudder was knifed an' dumped,
he moved righd in widda fleeda cars
an' thinned out Castrioni's gang
like he was Mister Death.
We watched 'im, maybe two hours lader,
dancin wid Rosabelle,
cool an' easy under d'chandeliers.

But soon I got t'thinkin
nobody should be peuifect

like Rocco is. It's kinda
hard to explain—like he was made
real good, only dey decided
d'human bit would take too lawng.
So den I blew. It shooer is different
away from town, widout no hoods er cops,
everythin slow an' simple. Some days
I feel I got no edges, den
it's nice alone up here
er talkin friendly. I guess
Rocco could change like me, if dey haven't
gunned 'im down. I'd tell 'im
bein tough an' smard an' rich
aint big: y'godda think some mower
an' feel de edges goin.

A WALKOUT

Back from the Far East
you spoke for being courteous
even at the price of hypocrisy.
I understood, agreed (not *quite* agreeing).
My favourite is 'All things are Buddha things'.
But we know the golden rules
are measures only, and later on
the drinks helped to prove it.
You cut from thought to person,
went for what you saw as
me and my way of thinking
till all my words were wrong. How could the calms
of Gautama or Confucius hold me then?

CONTEMPLATIVE POLITICS

The One and the Many, Atman, Dao,
the Plenitude and the Void:
these old familiars haunt me as I jab
the fork down deep, wrestle to budge
the roots of dock and bramble, lever a tough
fibrous clodge at the fern's foot
to uphold the rose's tenure. Whatever unity
lies at the heart of things, there isn't any

here on the plane of striving inscapes—
plant competing with plant, and shapely spikes
doing fearsome radical work. My will delights
in every stab of the fang-like steel,
yet feels the hurt to other parts of the Self
and begs forgiveness. False? Nothing is false
but a heart grown cold and separate. Sorry, nettles.
Sorry, worms, that prongs make tunnels
too, then shatter your underworld. I've just
by accident flipped a fat one, wrecked the stodge
he-she was contented in. I wait until
she squeezes through the fence before I let
the tines resume their harrowing. What a task:
in the mind of Shiva there's no cost
to count, but maya is all too real
for us, trapped in the macroscopic layer
of being, in analytical consciousness.
Yet here it's futile to talk of sin
or anti-social behaviour: my tacit 'sorries'
have nothing to do with that. These docks and roses,
worms and birds (I see the beaks attacking
soft juicy refugees, cutting
some into wriggling scraps)—these and the likes
of me are being themselves on a bio-scale
of power and disposition. So I clip
suckers like long green worms; but first I pluck
their single bloom, twin to the delicate
rose you find in hedges. Better kill it
like this, gently, than finish it off as waste
in a miscellaneous bagful. Stinking of sweat
and weeds, boots muddy, fingers scratched, I place
the stem in a jar of water. Before you sleep
I'll ring, my dearest, to tell you that I kept
as a love token the half-wild flower I picked.

GOING FORWARD BACKWARDS

My favourite seat, beside the driver's cab,
was vacant, only this time at the back.
Objects a morning metro trip reveals—
the shiny rails, ruffled embankments, leaves
of tree and hedgerow, blood-red signal lights—
all flow away from me. In Maori style,
its logic unassailable, I face
the vistas of the past; behind me, safe
against discovery, where the long track curls
towards a city's heart, the future lurks.

A SLITHERY TALE

It's all about a most peculiar snake
whose circumstances couldn't have been sadder.
'Ribs are like rungs!' he cried. 'Oh, how I ache
to be a firm uncomplicated ladder!'

'It isn't in your nature,' he was told,
'but if you're well behaved we'll give you one.'
He promised he would be as good as gold—
then slept, as if to prove it, in the sun.

He woke transformed—no reptile, but a train
gliding along all day from town to town.
Alas, his ladder crossed an endless plain.
'This life,' he hissed, 'goes neither up nor down.'

So now he has a different habitat:
here children babble, here the dice-cup shakes,
and though his world is absolutely flat,
the game goes up the ladders, down the snakes.

Fretful beneath his harlequin disguise,
he broods over an image from his dreams—
a woman gazing with enchanted eyes
into a fruit tree where a serpent gleams.

But sometimes in a dark Orphean trance,
changing from snake to rivulet to flame,
he revels in the mystery of a dance
where flowing down and up feel just the same.

TO LAUREN NEWLY BORN
also for Jan and Eddie

Lauren, your name is lovely—
that *l* and *r* and *n*
a chime melting on water,
easing the hearts of men.

It comes from distant ages
when leaves were heavenly signs,
and Petrarch made it timeless
in passion-haunted lines.

After the sleepy days,
the suckling and the weaning,
you'll give it year by year
your own rich meaning.

I send you now, for love,
a song as small as you,
wishing you faith and courage
whatever life may do.

A WIDOWER TO HIS DAUGHTER
for Carolyn and Clive

All those months attending the clinic, learning about
your own body and the one curled inside,
how to take care of both and your mind also,
how to breathe and relax and push when the time came.
You were pleased it would happen where they had new ideas,
allowed the mother to choose her own position:
you would enjoy it all. But the baby stayed cosy,
still wasn't budging a long time after its
hoped-for birthday. Now your blood pressure
is up, there are traces of protein in your samples.
You must go where the little one will be coaxed out:
everything will be harder, the pain worse,
that long preparation partly wasted.

I remember, though not as well as I should,
being with your mother when you arrived,
and find myself angry at the gods' indifference
to her entreaties for you since a week ago—
but know how childish the thought is, neither life nor death
having ever been like our fantasies. Yet in a way
I'm praying for you, my love, and I'll give you this
when your own daughter or son is firmly out in the world,
in the caring arms of her/his mother and father,
and you are happy again after disappointment.

SPRING SONG
after Herrick

Fair daffodils, we feel so sad
    to think you'll shortly die,
particularly since we've had
    R. Dawkins tell us why.

Thank God his peppy pages weren't
    available to Herrick.
The poet might have nipped, or burnt,
    a captivating lyric.

Though you are gorgeous bits of stuff,
    deep down you're mere machines.
This charm lasts only long enough
    to benefit your genes.

We thinkers are the same as you—
    essentially, that is:
though Dawkins knows a thing or two
    your role resembles his.

From slogans to symphonic themes
    —the mind's genetic chains—
a culture's low and lofty memes
    proliferate through brains.

Although you're not memiferous
    you pass on information:
genes, by constructing you and us,
    ensure their propagation.

We're capable of passion too,
    but that is by the way.
What plants as well as people do
    is done for DNA.

Fairest of gene machines, you know
    we'd save you if we could;
but every living thing must go,
    and go, alas, for good.

FEBRUARY WEATHER
for Enid Radcliffe

Force eleven to twelve, the sleeted gales
are blasting in, heaving the Atlantic over
railings, toppling trees, scattering tiles
and chimney bricks. Freaked-out ravers,
they whoop from coast to coast, leaving townships
amazed and fearful. Bollards drown; the tops
of cars are islands, the lower stairs
a continental shelf, the fridge an iceberg.
Where buses growled, now there are dipping oars,
ferried families, odds and ends in the tug
of water sliding away. Homely aid
steams and clinks in the church hall,
while hearts beyond the care
of any improvisation mourn their dead—
the man driving exactly when and where
a torn-off branch came down, the girl snatched
by a wave that leapt the wall.
And here are flowers that reached
for shining air, not knowing how to tell
quiet from noisy winters. Now their delicate
bodies, white, purple, yellow,
point in the wrong direction, battered flat.

THE CHAIN OF BEING

Attracted by the fidget and the chirp,
a cat is eyeing a blackbird on his perch
deep in an apple tree. Her lifting tail
electrically writhes and flicks. Elate
with atavistic ravening, she walks
the paling like a rope, then, hooking claws
in bark, begins her stealthy climb. I know
the bird as if the garden were his own,
and he's the one I feel for. Why should pets,
now strangers to the jungle and the steppe,
be fondly understood when they attack
live meat as well as chunks of Kit-e-Kat?
Predictably, the feathered pal retires
by air, the furry one by land. All's right,
as Pippa sang—or is till panic tugs
compulsively at scores of tiny guts:
sharp cries attest a universal law,

the trees and bushes fill, and over all
except the Boeing miles above, where lips
are moist with mutton, peas, potato, pils,
I see the hovering hawk, whose majesty
is founded on the humble kin he eats.

PSALM

Praise ye the gentle creatures, including
the dark-eyed kangaroo,
who, when she and her babe are menaced,
puts her back to a tree
and fights the dingoes off with her valiant claws.
Also the king penguin, who stands
firm in the time of blizzards,
cuddling a little one between his feet.

Praise ye the wolf, the tiger, and the shark,
the buccaneering skua, snatcher
of infant penguins from the breeding grounds;
the Hawaiian frigate bird, who gobbles
the young of his own kind,
and the sweet-voiced finch of the same islands,
hopping bright and beautiful, cracking open
the eggs of neighbours for their delicate meat.

Praise ye with full heart the eternal
being whose cosmic play
is kangaroo and dingo,
penguin and skua, finches, frigate birds—
is individual keeping up the species,
and species perpetuating life,
and life, that holy terror, without respite
gorging ferociously on itself.

THE BAY

Tuning that vague shrillness
above the sea's hiss,
you make out cells of melody
like the raw, tentative
music of genesis.

Then you reach sand, look up,
see the whole cliff
tingling with birds, and hear
their jubilant clarinets
playing a single riff:

the only notes they've made
from resonance that stirred
in bluegreens and in sea-lulled
leathery fronds before
the first cry was heard;

that keeps in just relation
different kinds, and brings
old and new together—
cradling flesh in rock,
filling the air with wings;

and now coaxes out
from room and car, to breathe
the tang of origins
where fish rot on shingle
and poisonous waters seethe,

Sapiens—who moved
fast into his own
wayward history, generating
seeds of fire and language,
fashioning blades of stone.

Here he puts his eye
to sandstone chinks, gazes
into uncanny chambers—
opium visions,
Piranesian mazes—

like the intricacies
of self and memory,
by which he became aware
of death, invented heaven,
learned to plan and worry.

Programmed for work and play,
determined to feel free,
he browns oiled urban muscles
under the sky's grill
and rides the tainted sea.

Caved in the cliffside pub
he stares across the bay,
and hears piped music, over
the wild calls, lamenting
'What made you go that way?'

Cradling glass in flesh,
he feels his mind slide
back toward timeless codes
that taught eyes to observe
and wings to glide;

but is boxed in his car again
as the daylight dulls—
quick-changer and polluter,
leaving far behind
the algae, the herring gulls.

AT THE SUMMIT
for Jeanne Harvey

Campi Flegeiri? Vesuvius? You preferred
the catacombs of Rome.
I understand; but graves and reeking vents
give you the full circle,
whose continuity then elides
both endings and beginnings.

That labyrinth was man-made, yes,
but formed, like the convoluted brain,
the small green lizards flicking
on slopes of tufo, the broom
flowering where ashes fell,
by constant replication.

It's disappointing, after the slow climb,
to find the crater dry as death,
filled with volcanic debris.
No pouting mud or sighing fumarole
hints at the awesome fires
of genesis, growth, survival.

But think how close we are
to turbulence, and so
to a strange order, something we couldn't see

though the pit boiled and flared:
graces and infinite repetitions
no maze of tombs can equal.

THE STORY OF LIZ AND FREDDIE

When Liz, who longed to become one flesh
with a superstar, believed she was on the shelf,
the gravity of her grief quite overcame
     the pluckiest effort she could make
to keep her nuclear pressure up. In short,
she lost her flames conclusively as a torch
     being doused: collapsed, imploded, was
abruptly the saddest something you never saw,
a vacancy set in the vacancy of the sky,
     with a density at the centre the likes
of which could never be found in any spot
on earth or another planet—a grim fullstop
     that made with the fall it ended (the sort
far loftier beings than Liz endured) an astro-
nomical exclamation mark! Or so
     it seemed till a big blue star came close
and showed the dot could be doubling, so to speak,
as a colon. Fiery Freddie just couldn't keep
     away from Elizabeth, who in turn,
for several years disconsolate and inert,
felt shivers of expectation. So commenced
     an orbital courtship dance, the dense
mysterious dark and the ardent light each taking
gravely the other's passion, reciprocating
     the yin, the yang, until the siren
drew the stranger across her event horizon
and thence to her singularity, where each mite
     of his teeming energy slipped from time,
space, objectivity. Thus, by gorging the zil-
lion particles of his substance, longing Liz
     became one flesh with a superstar
who had accidentally taught her the baleful arts
of the femme fatale. But what of the crypto-colon?
     Was Freddie reduced to nothing? No!
At any rate it's a claim worth taking note of
that all his engulfed remains, from quark to photon,
     found at the vanishing-point a hole
of infinitesimal size—beyond it, lo!
a quantum bardo, half hell half paradise,

    and finally, on the other side
of that nowhere-nowhen, a universe next door
to ours, into which tempestuously they poured
    to start a quasar. And Liz? Being left
unloved again in the larger void, she felt
as sorrowful as before, so it's good to know
    she'll finish powerfully when she's grown
quite small by evaporation. Better at least
to die with a starlike flourish, partly to steal
    away as a gentle gas and merge
one day perhaps with a plant-cell or a germ,
than suffer, deep-dungeoned in yourself, an odd
    no-longer-being that just goes on and on.

STARS

'They're so cold,
so far apart and single,
burning in icy distance
and going in circles for ever.
They don't give a damn for me
in the huge dark emptiness.
I don't give a damn for them.'

'To me they're close and friendly.
They're touching my eyes right now—
even those that are dead.
What they're made of never dies:
it's what you and I are made of,
so fine that it's almost nothing,
filling the whole of space.'

WHOLENESS
the EPR effect

Improbable? Then try to snip
the ethereal filament that joins
two particles of zero spin!

Tell me not only how it is
that every change to right or left
is answered by its opposite,

but also how a spinner knows
each new direction though its twin
has flitted to a far-off zone—

and knows it instantly. The speed
of light itself can't emulate
what happens in the timeless deep.

That inference made Einstein seethe.
Non-local causes? We disturb
the root of reason, granting these.

But others weren't upset at all,
for human partners likewise give
the slip to mechanistic law,

and some, if patience starts to warp
and wills go wandering, maintain
a superluminal rapport.

HOW IT ALL BEGAN

Risen from chaos, Atum stood
    resplendent on a heap of mud.
No consort helped him start the world:
Shu and Tefnut, a misty pair,
    arrived by means of hand and rod.

A shallower tale, though just as true,
    says Atum spat, or sneezed perhaps.
Those twins, whose coupling would engender
Geb and Nut, the earth and sky,
    were issue of the watery lips.

Intellectuals, though, denied
    that Atum needed blasts or spurts.
Having not only lips, but voice
and body too, he formed the gods
    by naming several of his parts.

For Memphite thinkers it was Ptah
    who, doing the job with heart and tongue,
conceived, uttered, inspirited
the whole mélange—'all gods, all men,
    all beasts, and every creeping thing'.

Now God ejaculates again—
  but how, with neither mouth nor glans?
What narrative can reach beyond
the point where time and space dissolve
and final mystery begins?

THIS BE THE CONVERSE
after Larkin

They buck you up, your mum and dad,
  or if they don't they clearly should.
No decent parents let the bad
  they've handed on defeat the good.

Forebears you reckon daft old farts,
  bucked up in their turn by a creed
whose homely mixture warmed their hearts,
  were just the counsellors you need.

Life is no continental shelf:
  it lifts and falls as mountains do.
So, if you have some kids yourself,
  they *could* reach higher ground than you.

HOLY, HOLY, HOLY

Clear air, clear water, spires above the meadows.
Four centuries away from gigs and demos,
rapt music filled the chancels and the naves
and flowed like thermals past the weather vanes.

In sooty boroughs hymns began to march,
to edify, to comfort, or to charm—
sustaining wills intent on paradise,
pushing all misbegotten doubts aside.

Today the striding rhythms are bearing sieges
by bouncy ones: here comes another Jesus.
The pillars feel a huge atomic lattice
quake in the trendy vibes, and long for Tallis.

UNCLE'S ADVICE

God? Come-come, dear boy,
you'll have to change your stance.
Believe in something *real*—
like History, or Chance.

THE THINKER

'Morality? Unreal—a marble statue:
the authority of your dad still getting at you.'
'So how about what Hitler did to the Jews?'
'Well, I guess we all have a right to choose.'

AFTER BUMPING INTO X YET AGAIN

O Lord, who art man and woman, girl and boy,
the quark, the clay, the earthworm and the rooster,
preserve us from, but let us still enjoy,
leftwing equivalents of Bertie Wooster.

TOWARDS LIBERATION

If chance competes with karma in deciding
whether we do more clambering or sliding,
let's hope that in the transmigration stakes
the ladders aren't outnumbered by the snakes.

ON NOT TAKING A PLEDGE

My reasons for declining taxed his brain,
but one of them at least may settle there:
for still, each time he goes to bed with Jane,
a rich tattoo avows his love for Claire.

A NUMBER TO BE PROUD OF

I've shed the name that I was lumbered with
for thirty-seven years. You've guessed it: Smith.
At last I am incomparably me,
the one and only Nine-six-two-eight-three.

FIGHTING WORDS

'This year we plan to show what men are worth
by having *Mother* Christmas in the shop.'
'I know—so we're installing Father Earth
to prove that they can make it to the top.'

STAR QUALITY

it's kinda like y know we jus do our own
thing n that's really good cuz we're always
tryin somethin new I mean we sorta go
all over the world only it's not the
money it's usin yr talent sweatin blood
under the lights n there's y know all those
people out there who love y like crazy n
y've had some big hits so y're where it's at
bein an artist makin the reviewers
rave n havin yr talent reckonised
I mean like y've arrived so y jus keep on
goin it's brilliant cuz now we've started
workin on a bran new album n I mean
yeah we get on really great together

THE BUTTERFLY EFFECT

Yes, oh yes.

Who could disagree
she's the one for me?

Briefly, the third time we meet,
I feel there's something not quite right;
but that's mere static—no need to fret.

The fourth time there's a tension it's hard to find
a reason for. I sense an unvoiced complaint.
Something I've said? done? haven't done, perhaps?
Ignore it. She may be tired. It's sure to pass.

The fifth meeting reveals a divergence of social outlook
that may reflect, I'm afraid, a temperamental difference.
I make a desperate effort to keep the gap from widening,
to choose unprovocative words without collapsing into
hypocrisy or surrender. We manage not to quarrel.

On the sixth occasion we're drinking wine. My hand wanders a bit
though not too freely, and later I say a little about my hopes
for a deeper friendship, and speak with the utmost delicacy of several
ways in which a man like me and a woman perhaps like her
might go about the deepening. She withdraws slightly—swims
a stroke or two, as it were, towards the shallow end of the pool.

The seventh time we're together I use the wrong word and she accuses me
of saying something I swear I didn't or at least that I certainly didn't mean
and she says I did and I say I didn't and she insists that the word I used
means one thing only and if ever a word existed whose only meaning
    was clear
beyond any doubt it was this one and I'm a brute and I say I'm not
    and anyway
what about what she said ten minutes ago yet I didn't object and I find
    myself
picturing her and me together a year from now and thinking
    no, oh no, definitely not.

A REUNION

1

I sing, not the sofa, but the bed—
and no four-poster proudly canopied,
    fit for a room in Hampton Court,
but one where lovers who'd been long apart
    were free from all formalities.
A quiet hotel our home for seven days,
    warm sunshine at the end of March,

Vivaldi and Bartok in the parish church,
    a stroll beside the Thames;
meals in the Moss Tree, coffees, beers, ice creams,
    a bookshop like a treasure cave.
No sightseeing duties this time, but a weave
    of memories, hopes, ideas,
and, while our window framed the blossom, hours
    of intimate affection—minds
and bodies, 'true plain hearts', responsive hands
    revealing self to self. Here
was the rich centre, the learning how to share
    all we'd become: and so
Bed is to be my subject, set by you!

2

    I'd spare you the history bit
even if I could cope. But let me write,
    ignoring briefly what you meant,
a line or two to celebrate the scant
    or sumptuous inventions
used by recumbent *homo sapiens.*
    Honour, my love, the pile of straw,
the mat, the cradle, the cot, the bed settee,
    the bunk and the four-poster,
the prams, the pudgies filled with air or water,
    the beds of nails, the hammocks,
the camp beds, bags, newspapers, cardboard boxes,
    the mattresses with stuffing
or bouncy springs, and finally the coffin—
    though, when this rots, the bed
remains that once was fashioned by a spade,
    now undivided earth
charged with the subtle power of life-in-death.

3

    The cue for *carpe diem!*
And so we did, but thinking of a poem
    by Donne, not Marvell—little rooms
instead of songless vaults and raping worms.
    Who could have been more free
from young anxieties than you and I?—
    so far apart in age,
yet twinlike in an ageless kind of knowledge
    affirming hearts distil
patiently from the mix of heaven and hell
    that all existence is.

Being hopeful is one way of being wise—
    even in bed (to keep this theme
within the limits of the sub-sublime).
    When feelings wake but members sleep—
like cellulose in spring without the sap—
    the fretful will's a menace,
changing mere disappointment to distress.
    Green-fingered, so to speak,
but far from green, you worked your magic like
    a tender and accomplished wife—
and had from me in turn, for root and leaf,
    the care that any man would give
who loved the person in the shapes of love.

4

    Meanwhile, what better way
to pass the uncontracted hours than lie
    peacefully side by side,
to drowse, to talk, or, pillow-propped, to read
    aloud or watch the box.
Those free-flowing conversations!—childhood, sex,
    music, the mystery cults,
political trends, and trendy architects
    like one we saw and heard
who didn't know that spires and arches soared
    and windows shone like jewels
for praise, wonder, a deep belief in souls
    and paradise and hell. How stunned
we were to hear cathedrals had been planned
    as 'information machines'.
But what can you expect when human brains
    are working on the kind
it's claimed will supersede them in the end:
    brains that will be—as ours
already are, so one conjecture goes—
    part vehicles for memes.
Likewise non-mental things, from chromosomes
    to bodies locked in love,
exist for genes (not species) to survive.
    I'd brought along the book where this
is argued out in detail, so precise
    and learned, yet so plain
that I could almost think of meme-machine
    as ultimately what was meant
by comrade, parent, artist, scholar, saint—
    all of them gene-machines as well,
like swan and lion, oak and daffodil.

But you'd have none of it:
you just ignored the book, and you were right.
  I thought of how you loved
your Carlo and Roberto, how you grieved
  in hospital when they were left
abruptly friendless, mewing for your soft
  caresses and their food;
then of the well-judged articles that showed
  how strong your feelings were
about all-elbow types who didn't care
  if pigs and poultry were abused
so long as priests and politicians raised
  no eyebrows. Dawkins, though,
would wish you luck: 'Pigs are machines, it's true,
  but so are women. Then
let's grant that pigs can feel, since women can.'

5

  One world, the all-in-all
of lovers, here and now a perfect whole.
  The idea's charming, yes,
but out of keeping with an age like this—
  with any, perhaps, except
the Dream Time. Well, romantic hearts have slipped
  closer to that unearthly state,
though buoyed on waves of sensual appetite,
  than normal times allow;
but nothing rids us long of what we know
  about the world outside,
or of our wish to know it. When we made
  love's music—hands playing
on bodies as on harps—we were denying
  all but the one desire,
and so enjoying one kind of everywhere;
  but little rooms become
a different kind when scenes from Moscow, Rome,
  Beijing, Pretoria, Prague
render a big world small, or a small one big.
  Now, nearer home, smashed windows,
flames; blood that could thrill to soft glissandos
  dripping beneath the strokes
of fist and baton, the blows of hurled bricks.
  'Community charge'? Why not.
The pun's a lesson: outrage will be met
  with rage—though Thatcherites
would fault the application. Then the slates
  flung from a prison roof,

sharply declaring that enough's enough—
    the overcrowded cells,
the slopping out, the anachronistic rules.
    And *Who Bombed Birmingham?*
reminded us of terror: first the grim
    expedients of the lawless,
then the tricks of unprincipled police—
    or so the suspects claimed
whom verdicts now debatable condemned.
    Another film we saw,
making our flexiworld (so safely) grow
    in time as well as space,
was *Lawrence of Arabia.* In a trice
    my age was roughly minus ten,
yours about minus thirty. So the sun
    blazed on velvety miles
of sand, heroic tribesmen charged their camels
    at Aqaba, and a mind half-mad
from double injury turned to taking blood
    for blood a hundredfold,
pausing before Damascus.—Oh, what wild
    propensities interbreed
to make the impassioned courtesies of the bed!

6

    Sad on the last night,
we found relief in music: first your sweet
    solo, that Russian lullaby,
then shanties, waltzes, marches, jigs—with me
    supplying the oompahs, you
the drum (your shapely back!), until the flow
    of song was mixed with laughter.
Thank you, my dearest, for that final gift
    from a never dying source—
the run of simple melody, simple verse,
    good sounds to go to sleep on.
Come daylight, dreamy consciousness would open
    to flint necessities
leading towards the parting of our ways;
    but meanwhile we'd be close and warm,
    the darkness gentle in our eyes,
your heart beating softly beneath my arm.

A BALLAD FOR THE LADIES AT YULETIDE

D'you think a man intent on song
should send his Christmas cards?
Then find a mate who's like a gong:
keep well away from bards.

Here's one who scribbles half the night
and sleeps when the sun is shining.
His boots and socks are a fearful sight,
his coat has an orange lining.

He thrives on cigarettes and beer,
on crisps and salted nuts.
His arguments are far from clear,
being full of ifs and buts.

He knows his lady cannot err
and he should be her minion,
yet he insists on vexing her
by having an opinion.

He overlooks, this addle-pate,
the rule that's paramount:
when a good woman helps her mate,
what *he* wants doesn't count.

He won't decry the furnishings
in other people's houses
(including hers), or sneer at things
like skirts and frocks and blouses;

but when, poor innocent, he hopes
she'll show the same politeness—
forgetting women have, like popes,
a God-implanted rightness—

and she, alas, lays down the law
about his dress and dwelling,
he groans like wood beneath the saw
and feels his heart rebelling.

He says, when she'd select his ties,
his bed, his bathroom mat,
'Let's look for one that satisfies
us both, and plump for that.'

But why should such a lofty being
concern herself with reason?

It's plain enough that disagreeing
is little short of treason.

Her vassal then, denied the balm
of tolerance and affection,
must conquer every loyal qualm
and opt for insurrection.

Come Christmas, much to her dismay
this desperado dares
to put his tree in a window bay
and not beside the stairs.

Possessed by some unearthly force,
her soul a blaze of fury,
she judges him without recourse
to advocate or jury.

She says 'It drives me to despair:
you always disagree!'—
and he, 'Did I advise you where
to put *your* Christmas tree?'

So pleads her unregenerate bard,
the maker of this song.
Beware then, ladies: life is hard
unless your mate's a gong.

A FRIEND IN NEED

Fortyish, finely rounded, with creamy skin.
I guess it's money she wants, but also the usual
conversation and plenty of strong black coffee.
'I'm freezing cold,' she says; but when I suggest
a chair by the radiator, she smiles and goes on
using the one she's in. 'Are you any good
at massage?' I hesitate now, beginning to get
a surprising picture. 'Why? You mean you'd like me—?'
'My shoulders, the back of my neck, I thought perhaps—'
'I'm afraid I'd do it badly.' We tread for a while
on firmer ground, till she says again 'I'm cold'
and speaks of feeling lonely, of wanting a man
who'll really care. The best I can say to warm her
ends in regretful silence. She drains her cup,
starts on a cigarette, and enquires abruptly

'Do you use condoms?' I laugh, tell her that's something
I've never been asked before, then quietly explain
there's someone else, and though we're lovers we have
no further need, thank heaven, for such precautions.
If I were free and a good bit younger—well,
it would have been nice; but given the way things are ...
'I see'—a small sad smile—and a little later
we cross the park to the High Street, where I draw
enough to keep her going. She thanks me, swears
it won't be wasted, offers to cook a meal
for me and my lady friend. I walk back home
safe and on edge, alone in wintry sunshine.

THE SHUTTLE
750 subjects were hypnotised and guided back to a state just before birth ...
Only 26 per cent looked forward to the coming lifetime ... 'It was something
that had to be done, like washing the floor when it's dirty.'
                                        —J. Fisher, *The Case for Reincarnation*

Heaven? They say it's wings and flamy curls,
or souls compounded with ethereal glue,
or even jasmine, sherbet, dancing-girls.
All wrong! It's being in Hartlepool with You.

See how, condemned to die a thousand lives
in Gosforth East, my tender soul is squashed—
how, Monday after Monday, it arrives
at weedy earth, paint peeling, floors unwashed.

I'll buy a prayer wheel, meditate and fast,
plough through Blavatsky, rise before the sun—
anything to be un-reborn at last
and live with my Incomparable One.

ANOTHER WEEKEND

Saturday night we're perfect for each other.
You're soulmate, mistress, daughter, sister, mother,
goddess, the lot. And when I hear your cries
of sharp climactic joy, I realise
there's still a mint of metal in the lode.
You can expect a sonnet or an ode.

On Sunday we're companionable too,
wholly at ease in all the things we do:
lingering, pillow-propped, to hear the news,
to sip and munch, to argue, chuckle, snooze;
having a pub meal, strolling by the sea,
playing music, reading, watching late TV.

Then our own little drama. 'Going to sleep?'
'Yes, I'm tired. Goodnight, love.' So I keep
my lust in check—but oh, tonight you wear
soft silk that leaves your legs and pussy bare.
'Prick-teaser!' Only joking. I caress
your thighs for comfort in the wilderness.

Waking near dawn, again I cuddle up,
fit snugly to your back, embrace you, cup
a lolling breast. You stir, I hear you say
'Move over, love—it's hot.' I turn away,
your well trained cavalier, and watch a cold
grey Monday slowly spreading, and feel old.

THE NIGHT SINGER

After that joy, a bird
was carolling near the window,
his tiny jets and rills of sound
clear in the dark stillness. We were charmed,
grateful, curious. Had we been awarded,
so close to docks and cooling-towers, the song
once heard in leafy Hampstead?

But all the twigs were bare! A robin then?
I saw his orange breast the next morning,
and now a book tells me
the glow of streetlamps, like the sun's,
will start his music flowing.

So there we are. But in another sense
where are we? Though the robin's tune
is fine, my love, and something to be proud of,
I feel, as you do, that our hearts have yet
to earn the nightingale's.

NOTHING LEFT

Oh this is vile, vile—
without your voice, your kiss,
to feel the heart grow sick,
to be but half alive:

each day this watery doom,
fine purposes that drown
in the compulsive round
of memory and mood.

I wonder how *you* feel,
since promises you gave
looked in the end so vague—
tormenting my belief

in you, in us, in ours,
reckoning weekend fun
companionship enough
though all my weeks were sour

with loneliness—that life,
whose late solicitude
went far beyond our due,
has closed a three-year file.

My love, you never felt
the same desire to snatch
what seemed a perfect chance,
and now there's nothing left.

A DREAM OF MARRIAGE

I heard a feminist on ITV
warning 'Beware your heart: your heart's a fool.'
How right she was. When Satan flattered Eve
she should have kept her head and stayed aloof.

More men than women use their brains, we're told.
Improbable! If thousands learn too late
(in Larkin's words) their special one's a dolt,
that seems another tall and godly tale.

The bridegroom's error shows that he's no less
a dolt than his beloved—or desire
so fogged his intellect that she could sell
(unknowingly?) her bum, her tits, her eyes.

Well, you're no fool, nor was it just your face
and figure proved me normal: you, entire,
were what disturbed my reason. No man's safe
whose heart persuades him that he's met Ms Right.

Divorced, wary, you knew how far to go,
allowed me parts of you and promised more,
but, scared of finding me a second rogue,
kept love on thermostat at slightly warm.

Too shrewd a female here, too fond a male—
too little heart, too much! Our progress looked
the sort the lame make propping the lame,
and lurch by lurch my optimism cooled.

Suppose I'd waited not three years but five?
Had levels evened—one going down, one up—
would they have made a husband and a wife,
or, passing, blipped inanely like a pun?

SILENCE

is fine if it's available
as no noise, though a sound
can be at home in it like
a bubble in still water.

But when it's a person not
replying, it makes you feel
a little, perhaps, like one
who knows he's slowly dying.

My address and phone number
both unused. But now, think-
ing of silences like hers,
I remember some of mine.

A WIDOWER'S PRAYER

God, I wish I could fall in love
unreasonably and absolutely.
Why must I keep on holding back
because every woman who comes along
is as flawed as I am? D is stupid,
J cockily clever. W,
stupid or clever, talks too little,
R incessantly. F is bossy
and L, I'm told, likes to be bossed.
G is flat where she should be rounded,
A is a hefty lass, and M's
face is far from being her fortune.
God, let me not be choosy, let me
plunge into unconditional love with a
woman as blessedly mad and helpless.
But what if you're truly a sorter out
(though not by the same rules), and men
are made irredeemably in your image?

THE DIVORCEE AND THE WIDOWER

Cool, guarded, she weighs him up. At least
that's what she thinks she's doing, but in fact
he's in the make-up chair: a standard Beast
is forming at her touch—the eyebrows blacked
and spread like raven wings, a shadowed stare
recalling one that drove her to despair.

Now every word he offers will attest
his patriarchal guilt. Her programmed brain
is satisfied that he's 'like all the rest'—
male-chauvinistic, lustful, selfish, vain.
He's trapped: for how would silence, or a smile,
go down in her interrogation file?

Though monster, he supports all human rights
and therefore women's—can even understand
why, made for popes and merchants, kings and knights,
expressions long in service are unmanned.
No wonder there's a boom in lesbian love
and heteromanticism gets the shove.

The trouble is—well, *isms*. Where they rise,
new dogmas and constraints replace the old.

He hints at such misgivings, but her eyes
assure him that the effort leaves her cold.
Then, in a pause, her image disappears
and memory floats him back across the years.

He sees a devil husband, one who dips
small bottoms and vaginas in the suds,
with creamy spoonfuls coaxes blobby lips,
shakes baby-talc on penises like buds;
who digs, repairs, paints walls and windowsills,
holds down a stressful job to meet the bills.

What if he told her that? Would she respond—
cancel the pointed ears, the fangs, the tail,
and, newly gentle, recognise a bond
between the female psyche and the male?—
or, unforgiving, grimly partisan,
despise him to the end for being a man?

AN AMERICAN WIFE AFTER READING *BRAIN SEX*

From now on she'll
be kinder. Though he sometimes talks like God,
often he suffers dumbly like a dog
tugging against the leash.

More Hyde than Jekyll
is what men are by nature, as old-timers
have always said. Even the ones with miters
are nowhere near angelic.

It's in the womb
that masculine and feminine divide:
all humans act—or should—as dolphins dive,
birds hop, or cattle moo.

Women are made
for things like loyalty, deep affection, em-
pathy, wifehood, motherhood. For men
there's nothing like a dame.

How can the schism
be healed so long as manly instincts tend
towards roosterishness? (Said the President,
retaliating, 'Tell that to Mrs

Coolidge please,'
hearing there was 'a new hen every time'.)
Still, after Moir and Jessel, husbands might—
just might—help wives to sleep

more sweetly: soothe
their hearts with gentle intimacies, try
to accept their joined up thinking (left and right),
though they themselves enthuse

with single track
assurance over cars and things. At least
one husband's trying. He used to be like steel—
almost an autocrat.

PASTORAL

For years we've loved and trusted you
as teacher, manager, doctor, nurse
and all the rest. You were the flow
of life, even its deep source,
once the goddess with horned brow
who framed the pharaohs' universe.
Archaic stuff—yet, seeing you now
at the wheel, I like to think the bus
responds as plants and creatures do.
Proudly, over that unisex
no-nonsense kit of navy blue,
your hair still ripples long and loose.
You set me down where apples glow
and epitaphs are blurred with moss.

A WAY WITH WORDS

'Gaudy' I said. Fool. It gleamed
with a shade of blue I love
and was close to her, almost, as her
shower water had been.
Something like vivid was what I meant—
not hard to explain, you'd think,
when softly she protested.
Or how about 'What I had in mind
was the original sense'?—poetic plea,

concern with hidden metaphor. No,
pedantic. Anyway false unless
the choice had been iceberg-deep.
A pause, thesauric agony. 'Nice' I said.

EITHER WAY SHE'S NICER

'It makes me feel like a slut to know
I'm in your imagination when you're
drunk and lonely.' I think of her saying
those words, yet I never heard her say them,
and if she knew how she's in my mind
when that's the sober thought I'm thinking
maybe she really would feel low.

PUB NOCTURNE

I end up here because, back from town,
I hate returning sober to where
the small hours will offer nothing
but Channel Three and a double bed for one.
You told me yesterday,
among some saddening things about
my way of conversation compared with yours,
you like to sit alone in the dark.
Dear friend, how I envy you
that self-possession or self-releasing.

EXITS

Better a windy edge,
whatever pain cries in a
drop to abrupt oblivion,
than this: the engrossing
softness, every inch
following the feet down
slowly, slowly, till even
the brow slides under
and the surface
resumes its bland calm.

THE BREW

See how it grooms itself,
the cloudy two-way slide
ending in stillness
and perfect demarcation.

But when you drink, the
black depth and the creamy
head slip down together
and have the one taste.

DEVOTION

Neither a skull nor a deathly picture
is needed. Contemplate the dust.

For a nocturnal *memento mori*
be shrouded in stinking sheets.

When writing sonnets
regard the work of the spider.

Let not the still small voice
be jammed by the vacuum cleaner.

Persevere in neglecting windows:
weeds will become phantasmal.

To be at one with the cosmos, begin by
loving the entropy of paint and plaster.

OPTIONS

In a thicket of crossings out
a few shy meanings lurk.
Beyond the window
branches and leaves declare
roundly their firm red fruit.

I suffer then
the imagined taste,

and the blended flavours of
duty, laziness, contemplation.

Leave the apples alone.
Pick them. Leave them alone.
Wishes, excuses, doubts
hurt like a rough draft.

But memory winks—
the backdoor lock is jammed.
Released from choosing,
where can I turn to free
the deadlock in the mind?

PARQUETRY
for Peter Bennet

The floor, by that name or another,
is something which the ocean has,
and which—pure jasper, glass, or gold—
trembles to wingbeats and hosannas;
is what, when fortunes fail, drops out
of people's lives; what speakers hold
and hitters sometimes hit; what's often
thudded on with rod or boot
and, either way, with powerful feeling
when it is someone else's ceiling.

Our selves are floorless: down they go,
converging, growing subtler, till
they're cosmic soul and then the void
from which new universes well
in dreamy splendour. Meanwhile I'm
sufficiently myself to feel
lonely a little in a world
where everything is solid still,
so much the stuff of space and time
that frauds a yogi puts to flight—
fear and desire, those tiresome twins
who coax us into all our sins—
keep bothering me day and night.

How cheerful then to tread a floor
whose present meaning is 'You're welcome',
laid by my poet-friend and host

in fourteen days while winter weathers
played modulations on the moor.
It's homely as a tray of mother's
toffee, a square of buttered toast,
yet firm as gold, though shiny bars
aren't packed as neatly as these blocks.
A lovely job. But neither wood
nor metal, Peter, draws on such
a gift as you've applied for years
to things less widely understood.
Solid with solid interlocks,
the varnish gleams; but what appears
when you are fitting word to word
bears deeper still your Midas touch.

A SPELL OF CHURNING

Do poems please? Tom B assumes they oughtn't.
His own mythologise what makes him tick,
and how his rhythms go is not important
so long as they advance the rhetoric.

Riddles may come like marchers or like dancers—
but never mind: work hard at what they *say*,
and when you know (or think you know) the answers,
just throw the patterned syllables away.

1962

SACRILEGE
for Peter Bennet and Michael Standen

Bring a poem, a bottle,
and lots of Christmas cheer.
He did. Even a church hall
—TO RESIST EVIL IS WISDOM
competing with the windows—
would tolerate at a time like this
the spectre of Misrule, lapsarian whims,
maybe as an ungrand finale
all those poetic tongues, well oiled,
engaging 'The Pheasant Plucker'.

Already warmed, like the friend he came with,
by beer and conversation,
he downed, among smiles and melting eyes,
red, white, then drams
of burning gold: joined in praising
the generosity of a Scottish writer
present at least in spirit.

Shifted to a charmed oval
of chairs, watched with revised awareness
candles devoutly lit, the lights switched off.
Through his own haze of incense listened
to quiet voices reading serious lines,
then rose to make his contribution:
apologised for bringing the wrong poem,
inflicted it, sat down to a crackle
of kind forgiving hands.

As metaphor after metaphor loomed and faded,
he slipped from time and reason, lapsed
finally into demonic rage, and heard,
alien yet familiar, a voice recalling
a manse boyhood and Christian Endeavour meetings,
then damning obscurity, rhetoric, affectation,
conceding 'Maybe I'm stupid', later
chucking wildly into the other pan
'I've written three or four brilliant poems
in clear unstilted language'.

Arrogant bastard, lout, spoiler,
breaker of Orphic eggs—
in shocked sobriety wondering now
if the father was speaking through the son
or the son defying the father.

THE HEIRESS

'A living ... ' He shuts the vestry door,
sighs at his little quip.
'But then, what matters is the will'
he thinks, too seasoned now for shock or grief.
Kneeling wearily on the floor,
he hears the gusty wind, the rain's drip
on his crumbling windowsill.
'Lord, I believe; help Thou mine unbelief.'

Dull at first, soon he will summon
all the art he knows
to make his discourse plain and true,
illuminate the mysteries of the Word.
In the manse pew a young woman
fights for composure till her face glows—
gives the old man his due
for trying, but finds the enterprise absurd.

Her turn tonight. She has prepared
her heart in the *Coach & Horses*,
being dull at first. And now her voice
is flowing among the listeners, deep and warm.
Something a family once shared
comes ghosting through the stillness as her verses
smuggle a father's choice,
denied to meaning, into sound and form.

CURRENTS
i.m. Tony Baynes

You showed me your poem mourning
a friend who floated down the Tyne;
told me during our only walk,
the kinked flood briefly lit by sun,
about those black twistings
that hurt your mind year after year.
Last night the news came
of your soaked body: now
I think of words, bridges,
deadly waters finally coupling.

BIOGRAPHICAL NOTES (1901-1922)

Cocky duo—G
canary waistcoat, J
blackthorn and yachting cap.
Devotees of beauty scorning
rabblement. Poems veer
from namby pamby in a garden
—for each verse a vellum sheet—
to ballads of the brothel.

Swimming in snotgreen sea
below martello tower.
'Chippendale sticks, no pictures.'
Novelist, for his keep, does
Watts-Duntoning and housework.

Quarrels and fallout. Artist-priest
in cunning exile, disguised as teacher,
hornily adoring goddess
disguised earlier as chambermaid,
now swims in purple prose.

Hellenic lyricist becomes
champion athlete, learns to handle
lancet, joystick, people.
Respected surgeon and senator, rages
to find himself reborn
as brilliant but irreverent
entertainer in scandalous
novel's opening pages.

YOUR DAY TICKET TO EXPLORE THE REGION

Valid from 9.00 a.m.
Mondays to Fridays,
all day Saturdays
and Sundays, Bank
Holidays and every
day throughout July
and August.
Buy them from
the bus
driver or in
advance from
any PTE local
travelcentre.

This is
exactly how the
info looked on a
poster in
the metro.
i reckon those
responsible might have
homed it into a

mag (al-
ternative) if
theyd known.
Dont get me wrong i
like it.

UNCOLLECTED POEMS
(1947-1983)

THE MAKERS

The artisan didn't collect his gear and say
'What beautiful object shall I make today?'

The poet didn't fondle a phrase and gape,
and think 'What elegant structure can I shape?'

The artisan made a gatepost
so that a certain gate could be opened and closed.

The poet started a poem
so that a meaning could reveal a form.

The gatepost is itself, sturdy and straight:
precisely this gatepost for this gate.

The poem is itself, the form-in-content:
exactly these words for what was meant.

The gatepost is rough, distinct and lovable,
untouched by the purpose that made it possible.

The poem is plain, final, able to please,
clear of the hungers that made it what it is.

SPRING

All Spring is poured in this field;
light streams down the trees,
wind trying to spatter it, and a child
paddles in green-gold sunshine to her knees.

It is time's deception—
whose suave treachery takes
the devil's bribe with one hand, with the other
flings a jewel among the tinsel fakes.

Only a moment of sunshine
the leaves of holly wear:
the child will not know that this was the quick pearl,
sincere were the sun's fingers in her hair.

For swiftly time's tinsel
will flash and leave her blind,
desire toy with it while Spring is a gleam
of antique gold on a dusty shelf of her mind.

URCHINS

Patched trouser-seats and legs,
pegged like washing along the parapet,
for a moment have been discarded
by eyes that are small blue whirlpools
greedily drinking the rhythm of boys
who slit the amber of the canal
like ivory paper-knives.

They chatter the world away like froth
from their tiny shoulders. The secret is still unguessed—
a stagnant plash in the gloom
of those tenement skulls; square sockets
suck this glee to the cynical mirrors
that shape a face scooped out with pain ...
These are the merry tragedians.

CITY SPRING

The berg of winter crumbles in spring's bright surf,
and spring swims through the winter-emptied heart
till all its dread dissolves in a froth of leaves
and a dazzle of birdsong. Now the jubilant trees
burst in fanfares and brilliant peals of blossom
along the wind-sewn suburbs. In the park
dreams flower again, beside the friendly pond
where tree-reflections play their gentle harp,
and peaceful are the noonday eyes that watch,
through tiny cobwebs of rainbow in their lashes,
gulls on cushions of diamond water, drakes
all spruced in velvet, plaiting glossy ropes
of ripples, or unfolding into flight
and flicking back small scimitars of spray.
Birds, perky as piccolos, beaks upraised
to mimic the tasselled lips of fountains, sparkle
obbligatos for spring from every tree.
The city laughs, pelted with warmth and colour;
people and things drink from a lake of light,
and tall stone figures are warmed alive and longing
to stride into the sun's mythology.
And see how spring, with skies of naked blue,
wipes clean the cloud-blurred pane of the still canal,
and makes it shine for two snow-petalled swans.
And the mind takes afresh these glowing threads,

weaves them in its silent loom and spills
like a brook the polished cloths of April thought.

NIGHT IN THE CITY

Astonishment flares again
at the beauty of wind-strummed streets.
The wind wraps itself round me,
drags me along by the hair,
spikes water from my eyes.
How strongly tonight it sweeps
and leaps down the rain-silked pavements,
boisterous batters the air.
The muscular flags are flapping,
rolling around their poles,
the bunting claps its hands,
and flickering birds and leaves
are blown round the rocking trees.
Wrinkling pools make neon
flowers shake, cuddled
between the slimy cobbles.
My eyes glide down a vista
where the tall breasts of buildings
wear dazzling electric brooches
that thrill the air with light.
Below them, what a weave
and waver of tinselled traffic;
the buses swing huge mirrors
that flash and surge with flame.
People step red-hot
from neon-haloed furnaces,
with lightning in wind-ripped hair,
and nothing more strange than a man
who crosses the street, spearing
with folded umbrella, spurting
a jagged blur of reflection
on wet pink slabs, is a devil
in some fantastic ballet.
Bicycles crammed together
tangle their twigs of chromium
like bunches of silver brambles.
Beyond them a sleek saloon,
nosing into its berth,
does slippery tricks with scraps
of light, like a polished magician.

Even an old scraped tramline
along a shoal of cobbles,
granted its gift by the rain,
is wearing a yard of sunset.

CATS

Along back garden paths
they move like rivulets
with a glide of liquid muscle;
and look—when two converge,
a sudden whirlpool of rage,
a churning foam of fur,
a slippery after-ripple
of angry tails.

GOLDFISH

In an oblong nebulous world
they dangle like lumps of topaz
or luminous wax.
Languid petal fins
lazily brush the stillness
and a body glib as a ripple
probes the twilight.
Black pale-spectacled eyes
gape from a blunt face,
the lunate lips munching nothing
with glum complacence.
Wombed within the soft translucence
of numb steel-blue water,
only those shapes like polished brooches
glimmer, fluid as phantoms,
or bubbles, twirling upward
like bent and glittering sixpences
tossed by fingers of liquid,
trouble the milky-way
of an indigo sky.
This tiny world is dazed and dumb
with somnolence.

CONCERTO

Hear this rivulet flow
down chasms and crags of a dark accompaniment,
thrill with a shrill glint of sunlight,
smooth as an otter probe low
through tangled glooms of brake and glen,
polished to a silver harmonic, poise
a glassy film on rock's lip,
then steeply plunge with sweep of noise,
smash into cymbal spray, and slip
past glancing grace-notes of piccolo grass,
and sleek and quiet as a silk wind, slide
along firm sandbanks of the brass,
then swell to join the climax of the tide.

In us who listen,
it glides through the twisting channels of sense,
to pour into the deep heart's reservoir.
O feel its fullness, feel the heap of dense
ton on ton of limpid music flood
these empty acres of longing, until blood
itself is music jetting in every vein,
and all this tightening sound, this glittering weight,
must shatter its towering dam and inundate
the placid fields of logic in the brain.

RHAPSODY A LA RODGERS

Such a surging surf of, shifting shingle of leaves,
lather of leaves in the sweeping swell of the storm!
Such heaps of foliage rocking like crazy crowds,
and pan-expansive hands all washing in wind,
shovelling up slithery sun-suds! O what piles
of pugilist-punches, enormous dormitoryfuls
of pummelling pillows! What orchestras crammed with harps,
landslide glissandos flung down mountains of music,
swimbel and swish of cymbals! What a tipsy
trip and topple of topers, and Falstaff-affable
bellies belching! O what a lock and lunge
and lurch of wrestlers, bashing of battering-rams,
dynamite-dunted dykes! What a rugby-rumple,
scramble of scrums, scuffle of coal in scuttles!
Such polka-plunges, rumba-wriggles-and-rolls,
barn-dance barging, flinging and flop of flounces,

bouncing of bustles ! What banging bundles of bells,
squashing of cushions, squelch and slosh of galoshes!
What dollops of dough and jolly joggling of jellies!
Such a labour of lungs to bulge the bellies of bagpipes,
quaffing and chaff of laughing cavaliers,
swan-bosoms busy at bossing of brazen boys!
What a jumble of jolting jumbos, whacking of whales!
What wind-paunched hammer-o'-slack-punched windjammer sails!

All these become kith and kin behind Fancy's fence
when he feels facetious amid this tussle of trees;
and I bind and gag for a spell the blue-pencilling censor
who sits at a desk in my intellect, waiting for Fancy's
impulsive pratings, toiling for tyrant Taste.

But here comes the spittle-spatter of rain. I run
to under a tree's umbrageous branch-umbrella,
lean on the trunk, look upward into the leaves,
and wish that I were within this sinewy wood,
tangled in tempest, ripping the rope of wind,
paddling bare feet in chainmail shallows of shadows,
with hoards of leaves torrenting over my knuckles
like nickels in silvering sunshine, and score on score
of twigs a-twisting, intricate, intimate all
as a wrist-watch heart!
                              And when the rain has passed,
back I go to glow in the broom-wind's business
and feel it sweep out words like crumbs from a crack
deep in the mind, to wind-winging wand them birds.

ICARUS

See how, lightly tilting, the ivory blade
slits the smooth-drawn cellophane of morning,
when easy as a seagull and unafraid

the young fool soars to taunt the sunlight—scorning
all fates and fetters hostile to his will,
chucking into the wind an old man's warning—

swims upward through the sluicing air until
the sun sucks and nibbles at the straps
binding his wrists and shoulders, and they spill

warm wax like threads of blood. The taut wing snaps,
slides away like an avalanche. Limbs cartwheeling,
the gay daredevil ace flounders, flaps

like a wounded bird, the bells of panic pealing
crazily in his skull, his skyhigh wonder
shattered like glass—sees cloud and water reeling,

and gashes into lunging mounds of thunder.

SNAKES

I can't say whether real ones
swallow their own tails—
or, if so, whether the shape they make
is anything like a circle.

Nor do I know if there's a myth
where one swallows another.
Sometimes I feel that if there isn't
perhaps there ought to be.

In the case I heard of, though,
a real keeper really arrived
in time to catch the tail
and pull the whole lot out alive and wriggling.

NATURAL HISTORY

In a room like that, if you dare to enter,
a light will give small comfort—
will show you exactly why
the carpet is shifting and whispering
on its underlay of guano.

About the flitter of wings
and the voices thin as needles
you will already know; and perhaps you'll find
equally unsurprising, however weird,
the black torrent that pours out into the night.

Close-ups are even worse.
Gargoyle masks—all snout and jag-toothed grin,
rucks and nodules of furry rubber—
are pinned between the outsize ears
by small glittering eyes.

And the skeletons,
with elongated arms and fingers
bracing their leathery capes,
look enough like ours
to make the difference sickening.

No wonder our depravities grow wings
in caves seething with snakes and insects,
and flap in the moonlit murk
of myths and horror films,
nightmares and DTs.

Codswallop, of course. We all know
that ugliness is in the beholder's eye,
and if only we could see aright
those canny little creatures
superbly adapted to their environment,

etcetera ... No doubt if we changed places
and one of them wrote *Paradise Lost,*
Satan traversing chaos
would be a barrister with a fine profile
who drives to court through sunny streets,

returns at dusk, triumphant though fatigued,
to a villa beside the Thames,
and pours himself a scotch
in a well-lit centrally heated lounge
with a perfectly fitted carpet.

INVASION

At half-past three the enemy arrived.
Excitement spluttered along the line of watchers
winding like a fuse to the circus ground.
The suburbs scarcely knew why they applauded
the loud-mouthed tubas and the squawking clowns,
the coloured caravans and in parenthesis
the arrogant beauty of women's breasts and thighs
offered with such a handsome lack of scruple.

The long-faced houses standing in shocked silence—
blinds half drawn against the promiscuous sunlight—
scowled on the welcoming laughter of the truants,
and wondered why this dangerous upheaval
so smacked of *joie de vivre* and liberation.

LANDFALL

This is the final aim of every voyage.
Though the young man may run away to sea,
the wind blow dreaming embers into flame,
and under shrapnel spray his body harden,
a tough joy clench his teeth, you will not find
in love of this the motive, though himself
and all the world should think so. Each brief exile
tunes his blood again to a racy morning
when gulls flicker and squeal around the masts,
the small flags lick the breeze, and the crew
with darkening eyes watch the bows glide home
into the welcome of the harbour's thighs.

THE SEA

I stood by the window on a storm-lashed morning
and looked out beyond the desolate trees
with white berries of rain, at the hulking sea
that went berserk and slammed on rock, scrabbling
the shingle beach, and heard the slithering gulls
echo a squeal of hinges through the mist.
Loneliness and fear had flowed in, breaking
across my mind, and in the mist of memory
recalling days once spent on summer headlands
a gull cried out its strident prophecy.

And then a polished wind came slashing down
and cut the clouds to pieces. An arctic winter
blasted with spring, they crack and disintegrate
and slide away in slow majestic icebergs
over a flood of blue. Joy in those young days
had been blinding as iceberg clouds, spring come swarming
in gusts of light racing along the sea.
Yet always the shadow-blizzards swept them off,

and I had never learned to reconcile
dark and bright moving across my life.

But waited for those evenings when the water
is forged in pure silver, such a white
brilliance lights the soul all jagged splinters
of desire are melted down and cast again
and cooled into the image of the night;
when glinting waves along the beach are scything
the swift growth of time, and in the stillness
are only shifting swathes of foam to tell
of conflict at the edge of timelessness.

But now I know the caged mind can bear
no more than diamond glimpses of the moon:
the steady gaze is for another knowledge.
And I shall learn to wish no more than days
of light and shade answering to the touch
of the wind's whip, and what the groomed waves
with thundering hooves, reined up along the shore,
may bring of fragile gifts from lands of legend.

DEJECTION

Forgive this dark withdrawal that dissolves
your friendly laugh and all your eager words
as though I'd no desire to understand.
But take for pledges of my lonely wish
to break out of the shadow and be with you,
my blunt-edged answers and my awkward smile,
the glances improvised when sight means nothing.

This is an old sickness. It was this
that long ago locked me into myself,
made me afraid of people. But in new
environments I learned to challenge pain
and work it into a complicated pleasure,
another kind of agony. The world
that's known in common living I neglected.
People no longer mattered but in thought
where then I came to love them for the deep
roots of life plunging below the thorned
endemic code, the symptomatic gesture.
To shape immense beliefs, cutting away
the barbed-wire fence of every cramped, exclusive

loyalty—that was the mind's concern;
living, I chose myself for best companion,
escaped from people, from the deadly currents
that wrench the tide of feeling and opinion
rammed between rival headlands, and reduce
to early shipwreck or irrelevance
the accurate beauty cast for open seas.

But isolation is a bargain-driver;
I saw a fortune wasted, weeks and months
lavished on lust and idleness. So many
days were counted out in green places
for the rare vivid moments that reveal
colour and birdcall and the glint of water;
so many nights went down the drain for heartsick
wandering through the city's fetid mazes.
I say no more of that, only remind you
that I have tried since then to make amends.
No ivory tower I come from, but a blind
castle with stinking dungeons, to descend
into the crowded valley seeking life.
My darling, hold me fast with love when those
bleak walls and stairways, drugged with recollection,
invoke my will to be their desperate phantom.

NOTE FOR AN IMAGINARY DIARY

Once, to laze the weeks away like this,
stealing a moment more of truancy,
another after that on the slightest pretext,
seemed allowed or even willed by God—
yet needed no doctrine of predestination.

Somehow, it seemed, nothing could go far wrong.
Well, if it wasn't God's idea, at least
a job not done, a fear not overcome,
an easy pleasure seized at the last moment
simply couldn't matter much in the end.

For this was Me. Whom some vague destiny
had favoured with a special kind of schedule:
so if I chuffed a while on sleepy looplines
or even jumped the track for half a day,
I'd still arrive at the proper place and time.

Playing hookey's dangerous now. But still
the sensual fool persists in quaint notions,
such as: knowing at last the risk you run,
will you have the guts to go on choosing
the loafer's way, the least exacting pleasure?

(How well the tempter knows the lyric poet,
who's never sure the fool is not the sage.)
When I would answer, two things bother me:
the highwire stretching from belief to action;
the fact, if such it is, that I am free.

UNIQUENESS

There is no way of measuring desire.
Who can say that here was a freshet's flow
and here a brawny wave shouldering rocks?
No search of history or legend will determine
that one passion, renowned,
was justified by greatness, while another
was commonplace, a hot infatuation.
Each had its own quality and its force,
and every nuance, like the latest touch
of the Heraclitean wind on moving cloud,
was secret and unique beyond all reckoning.

'Had I been you' means nothing.
Owlish advice, moral comparisons
will never serve either for different people
or for the rival selves in one person.
This heart and mind must always
baffle me their intimate companion:
make me wonder again, briefly gifted
with my own spring season, when brash sunlight
startles my eyes and a breeze flirts the leaves,
how winter was authentic or dreamy autumn
anything but a deep dissimulation.

CONSCIENCE

Red has its part to play.
Amber is fine so long as
they both give way.
When green comes I am glad.
But the red and the green together
drive me mad.

HUSBAND AND WIFE
for Muriel

I wonder why you said to me in your dream,
eight years after our wedding, 'Let's get married.'
The grace of blindness leaves me free to guess.
Was it refreshment simply, at the stream
of our first pleasure? A gentle, harried
plea? Or a cunning emblem of success?

You tell me the dream: you joke about it and then
forget: why drill for logic in the second
of those alternatives? The first is trite.
The third proclaims your shrewdness about men,
how calm and gay your love, how well you reckoned
possible ironies, tricks of appetite.

Married-love should be spelt with capital letters
only in dreams: is asked for only there
except by the wistful. Marriage awake is not
the loving, but the loving with all its fetters:
Aphrodite with curlers in her hair;
the house, the job, the pram, the garden plot.

In waking, then, most wisely you pretend
(This much your dream implies) we are no more
than friends and lovers. You keep my touching new,
my tender lust alight. The coin we spend,
worn smooth, retains its worth: in dreams you store
inviolate gold. I'm glad I married you.

WAITING

All over now. A week ago
you smiled indomitably through
a blur of pain. Our hands clutched
like meshing steel. I watched
her head budging, her dainty thigh
eased out, and heard her small prodigious cry.

She nestles, all nine pounds of her,
deep in my arms: a private stare,
hands neat as petals, the head I kissed
warm like a bird's breast.
The pleasure's mine: no frills assuage
her radical, uncomplicated rage.

No more than touching, glance, word,
can satisfy a different need.
In the fulfilled mother's eyes
the lover's fancy plays.
Waiting, I suffer this delight
of seeing more dryad in you every night.

BETWEEN THE DUTIFUL BLOWS

Between the dutiful blows
clanged on a mundane anvil,
you have found stars, and behind
the dollars a lurking lyric.
The inevitable saxophone,
luxury's orator,
constantly lubricates
the parched cracks of your senses;
you allow yourself to pretend
that across society's vermilion
grin, slinks no sour phantom.
But you will sometimes find
delight in midday parks,
maybe will see for a moment
trees that juggle with diamonds,
long grass muscled by wind,
a blue explosion of pigeons.
Hoard their beauty; hoard
the sunlight on beach and sea-foam
in summer days; the moon's

writhing silver on cinderella
waters along the factories:
when sinews have tired at the anvil
and sense-gathered burrs fall away,
these will be steel to startle
gold fire from the flint of your soul.

WORDS' AND VEINED MUSIC'S FLOW

Words' and veined music's flow
floods the ear like tide a whorled
shell, and whirled gusts of conception
come crystal and light as filliped snow.

Wind foams the pines that taper
crumpled rock to sky's blue pallor
cream-smooth; pillar and wall are creamed
in the sun, pulsed with a shadow's caper.

Sense perceiving these, the soul
is full, foregoes another troth;
intimate is truth in the fathoms of being
as water's cool mould to a bowl.

But sediment apprehension stirred
spews upward through limpid wonder;
desire must wander, thought flit
as, free or falcon-cowed, a bird.

THE CODEX READER

Small leaf of fire surrounding him with gold,
he searches thorny thickets of the mind
to gather all the nourishment they hold.
Then, for a moment, reasoning goes blind:
no longer hungering after how and why,
his will draws to the presence none can name,
like the rooted flow of a poplar toward the sky
or the stemmed burning of his candle flame.

THAT YOU FEEL JOY AND PEACE

That you feel joy and peace
looking at such things—
rivers and hills and clouds,
sunlight on distant wings,
and that you find in them
inklings of some unknown
unending loveliness,
this to all denials
asserts one simple yes.

That you feel pain and doubt
thinking beyond such things,
troubled by a phantom's
insidious whisperings,
or by a private grief
that drags you from the vision,
this is what makes you grope
for some precise illusion
concocting faith from hope.

THE BELLRINGERS

For ages beyond number the taut ropes
have drilled the ceiling, hand- and tail-stroke rocked
the bells into exploding eloquence.
Sixty giants who have pinned their hopes
high as the belfry stand with eyes locked
straight in sockets, dwarfed by the immense
ringing-chamber, feet sunk in a scree
of skulls and bones, or mires of rotting flesh.
Stagnant, the toxic air inflames their lungs:
even to breathe is torture. For them the free
wind has never whispered, nor a fresh
palmful of mountain water cooled their tongues.

Once in a hundred years there comes a giant
(others too, less gifted, replace the dead)
whose singing voice flows clear among the bells,
weird and prophetic, joyfully defiant,
rousing his partners for the work ahead.
There, in the midst of suffering, he tells
what strangely he has known of wind and rain
somewhere beyond the senses' reach. And so

the pendulum still swings—hope to despair,
despair to hope—and still their bodies strain,
impelled by one dynamic, and they know
their hearts can never rest or cease to care.

Some believe the soul will enjoy at last—
some that it will become—water and wind,
if they will ring strongly until they die;
many praise the singer, but are past
taking the message in; a few, thick skinned,
ring for the sake of ringing and deny
there's any truth transcending bells and bones.
But guesses make no difference: one intention
drives them all—to ring the changes well,
fighting against the acid overtones
that burn away the edge of their attention
fixed on the powerful strike-note of each bell.

Five teams of twelve, with minds to each other bound
by chains of metre only death can break,
they couple force and faith striving to build
five glorious alexandrines that will sound
in unison at last—and then the ache
will melt in wonder at a hope fulfilled.
Never will they attempt another change:
they'll ring relaxed, with no more thought than goes
to remembering, and safe within the known
release their minds to soar among the strange,
to swim in the ideal air that blows
across their dreams from that clear baritone.

Unimpressed, a few make speculations:
'Surely the ringers ought to have been primed
to follow the same sequence from the start.
Instead they've tried billions of permutations
to find a unison, sixty bells inchimed,
an ecstasy of bronze! And what can art
contribute where no order was agreed?
These halfwits wait on chance and yet they wait
with hope! But even if their wish came true
they'd just be bored, and make their masters lead
them off again into their former state
of crass resolve, where trial was all they knew.'

The singer looks in their disdainful eyes,
his heart going out to them and all the rest.
Through gloomy squalor, like a flood of gold
his noble music spreads to neutralise

the deadly overtones—or drown a nest
of dissonances writhing to enfold
the giants in a nightmare. Some, unnerved,
go mad and try to hang themselves, or burrow
into a heap of bones or stab their ears;
and those beside them grapple wills that swerved
for a moment close to paralysing sorrow,
then watch the ropes intently through their tears.

Into a sky of spring on a diamond day,
with sixty battering bells the frenzied tower
erupts its crude polyphony. A bird
glides on expert lyrical wings to play
a long glissando on a sunlit shower,
and there those wild metallic notes are blurred
into the softest fountain-fringe of song,
to fade at last in a breath of wind and rain.
Far below, the seer lifts his voice.
Wording a memory of his flight along
currents of limpid air, he sings again
to help the labouring brotherhood rejoice.

THE SCEPTIC

Because he said now one thing, now another,
as though he picked his thoughts out of a hat,
don't call him insincere or inconsistent.
That's what he would have been if each assertion
had tallied with the others; for in spite
of all his claims to independent thinking
he would have compromised to drug his spirit,
shying away from puzzling contradictions.

Only hypocrisy is measured out
in months and years, sincerity in moments.
There is more beauty in the hard, uncertain
trek through miles of unknown territory,
the slow sift of gravel and the few
wet crumbs of gold held in the rough hand,
than the fat thud of a safe-door on the fortune
inherited from a suave dyspeptic uncle.

ANGRY MAN

Behind his adult eloquence you see
the unreasoning assurance of a child.
Rather than pause, consider, disagree—
and risk being called half-hearted, vague, or mild—
he pumps his fury through a verbal spout
and jets it in your face. He makes immense
the trivial issues that he roars about,
equates intelligence with being intense.

All of us are fanatics when we're hurt,
and *no* becomes the murderer of *yes*:
if cleanliness insults, we worship dirt.
But in the name of freedom let's confess
thought lacks its finest passion until pride,
anger, contempt and fear are laid aside.

POINTS OF VIEW

Enters, in excellent voice, with ego glinting
wickedly, newly honed on a piece of scandal
or a unilateral chat with one of the meek.
Stoops on the first good nature unwary enough
to grant his presence, and stabs: 'A society full
of physical violence, and on the other hand
this namby-pamby talking: *I should have thought ...*
of course one has to admit ... de-da, de-da.
Now I, as you know, am dead against physical force,
but I'm all for a verbal knockabout—'

                   ' Yes, but surely—'

'I know what you're going to say: *there's a happy medium.*
But medium is mediocre, it's wishy-washy,
it's—'

         'Not so fast ! That wasn't what I intended.
I meant—'

         'What else could you mean? If a person's neither
this nor that, he must be a feeble mixture.
It follows.'

         'Does it? You're neither A nor E,
so you must be a diphthong?'

                                   'Exactly!—and obsolete
as *mediaeval* and *aesthete.*'

                         'You could be X.'

'X is a quibble.'

                         'It is to people who think
in twos—in opposites and amalgamations—
people who squander language in knockabout
and namby-pamby, and mediums happy or sad;
but X is real enough to those who wait
alone and watchful, searching out something new,
and using their voices not as weapons, like you,
but to give their egos the slip, and communicate.'

AN EXAMPLE FROM ULSTER, 1973

Republicans, Unionists (certain kinds),
Papists and Calvinists closed their minds
to the homely logic of moderation—
the surest way to emasculation.
'Ireland, unite!' one party cried.
'If you won't, you'll have to be unified.'
Others declared 'We love the Queen'
or 'You'll see no orange man turning green'.
Twomey caressed his gelignite
and muttered 'We'll *make* them see the light,'
while Paisley, impregnable as King Kong,
bellowed 'I'm right, so the Pope is wrong.'
The rifles cracked, the bombs exploded,
hearts were broken and coffins loaded,
until, in a civilised sort of voice,
experience warned 'You must make a choice:
either you follow the light of reason—
i.e. refrain from shouting "Treason!"
and give up thinking your point of view
is the only one worth attending to—
or you blow the country to bits with guns
(relying, as always, on your sons).'

Westminster, appointing Willie Whitelaw,
said 'You'll be treated like an outlaw.
These Irishmen are a crazy lot,
their tongues are loose and their heads are hot:

they're mostly fanatics, so if you're wise
you'll never say "equal" or "compromise",
but allow each party and sect to think
you agree with them that the others stink.
Don't be too nice or they'll call you smarmy,
and try not to mention the British Army.'
When Whitelaw sat them around a table
and proved himself humane and able,
Catholics like Clapper and Prods like Craig
said 'liberal', 'wishy washy', 'vague'.
(Alarmed that their sentiments coincided,
each argued 'You can't have meant what I did'.)
At length the more sensible ones agreed
their job was to answer a common need,
but the first debate in the new Assembly
might just as well have been held at Wembley.
Paisley (for Calvin, Queen, and Border)
kept interrupting on points of order;
the chamber began to fizz and rumble,
here a challenge and there a grumble,
till 'Heretics! Traitors! Fifth Columnists!'—
an explosion of prejudice, insults, fists,
boots, agendas, portfolios,
added a page to Ireland's woes.

Derry, Belfast, Armagh and Newry
are rocked by blasts of anarchic fury,
but nothing is solved: as the years go by,
factions and fictions multiply.
Innocent people walk afraid
as the news breaks of another raid—
scared to go near a parked car,
meet friends in a pub or a coffee bar,
fearing some indiscreet remark
may bring strange visitors after dark,
that they'll see a son or a husband shot
for what he is or for what he's not.
Republican Papists, Unionist Prods
both know that their point of view is God's;
in the ego's dark, where the world's affliction
is deeply rooted, an old conviction
sounds in the emptiness like a gong:
I am right and you are wrong,
I am right and you are wrong.

BOMBERS

The sirens, weird and sickening, made a smear
of harmony on the air, wormed back to hell,
and left a silence like projected fear,
a tranced alertness while the clouds were frisked
by searchlights; till at last, as though one spell
melted into another, came the drone
of engines built for death and devastation,
then the reports of ack-ack gun and shell,
the bombs' thunder ... But at least they risked,
takers of life, the losing of their own.
Distress became the root of aspiration,
and though two countries hated at long range,
backbiting neighbours found the heart could change.

Now war comes sneaking into cosy bars,
hotels and cafés; slithers neat and small
through letter slots, is parasite on cars,
or snugs down under quiet country lanes;
lurks in the shadow of a garden wall,
waiting for someone coming home to sleep,
and, visiting, leaves a husband or a son
crippled and bloody, writhing in the hall.
Through years of failure, while the spirit drains
out of a province, furtive bigots creep
in their own murk with gelignite and gun,
hoping that their guerrilla talk will blur
the hard black outline of the murderer.

OPPORTUNISM
based on a Reith Lecture

That the war may be continued
that there may be a steady demand for weapons
that research may be underwritten
that firms may prosper and grow large
that directors may be appointed
that expense accounts may be in order
that there may be scotches, cigars and handshakes
and swimming pools made of marble,

let the woman weep in the dust.

That the war may be continued

that there may be expenditure on weapons
that industry may flourish
that the economy may expand
that there may be a higher standard of living
that the electorate may be contented
that politicians may remain in office
and ripen towards their memoirs,

let the child die screaming in flames.

TWO VOICES

1

'Love for the human race'—the words
are glib yet doggedly sincere:
our holdings threatened, reason herds
old values, gets the boundaries clear;
the rest is vague at first—but still,
the argument requires we show
this favoured movement of the will
before we test the undertow.

The humanist approach implies
what we would like the world to be,
not that we idealise
the facts. It's true humanity
is easier to love than people:
currents of selfishness will grate
on stones beneath the gliding ripple,
until in self-defence we hate,
or self-disgust; with turn of tide,
surface and depth no longer move
against each other to divide
the chordal fathoms of our love—
which means perhaps that we are then
pleased with ourselves and glad to share
what pleases us. Nine times in ten
it seems experience will not bear
a spiritual analysis
(but wonders why it should), and hence
you ask why we will not dismiss
phrases that jar on commonsense.

That dreamed-of terminals remain
beyond our reach is no surprise:

by definition, to attain
the ideal is to realise,
then lose the antonym that makes
man's endless want articulate;
and knowing this his willing takes
the consequence without regret.—
Ideal objects may decide
our acts, replacing what we feel
(like anger's impulse turned aside
by reason, not a double deal).
But this, remember, works two ways:
hoping for such a love as men
of generous disposition praise
though knowing how time and time again
they miss perfection, we achieve
that gracious view of life which finds
it good to pity and relieve,
to cherish, not exploit, the mind's
ability to shape our deeds;
if you, observing how the goal
we aim at constantly recedes,
will simply dynamite the whole
aspiring structure of our thought
and build with facts, then it will be
exactly there that you are caught
by lurking unreality.
The 'realism' you prefer
can never give sufficient scope:
restricted loyalties will stir
uneasily, begin to grope
for imaginative *lebensraum*;
and, being distrustful when above
the outer wall they see those calm
horizons of ideal love,
will choose an arid wilderness
where pride and cruelty invent
a myth of glory to redress
their solitude, their discontent.

Close to the line where aims divide
the differences are hard to fix:
we might belong to either side,
so subtly good and evil mix.
The common preference is to drift,
but not too far, and cautiously:
the waves do little more than lift
the stranded keel of apathy.
But here again those restless powers

may one day float us farther out,
then which persuasion, yours or ours,
will end the aimlessness of doubt?
Though facts fall short, by them we take
the measure of what dreams have done:
to put it bluntly, yours can make
a Hitler, ours a Jefferson.

2

You have conceded more
to cynicism, with your tidal streams,
than I have either heart or reason for,
yet you would call *me* cynic. Then those 'dreams':
it's nice to dream, and may be useful too—
I wouldn't grudge you that.
But two dreams only? Was the line you drew
a lawyer's trick to make his logic pat,
or does it represent
a spiritual truth? I hardly know.
But such smooth argument,
sorting out con and pro,
tyrant and liberal, makes me feel that I'm
being tempted in a way,
especially when metaphor and rhyme
put on a neat display.

I realise, of course,
that you're afraid
this unimpassioned outlook may disguise
the muck on which a tyranny is made,
and think we'd better use
imperfect means than hesitate and miss
the opportunity to judge and choose.
All I can say is this:
If it means anything
I'm on your side,
but not for any reasons I could string
together on a platform. Say I tried
to analyse, evaluate and name
the rough, entangled motives of a man
willing to live, and ended with the same
uncertainty I had when I began.

TO A BLACK WRITER WHO DESPISES LIBERALS

1

Love as a mask for hate,
'reaction formation'. Excellent: play it hard.
It looks good, sounds good,
so easy to grasp yet spiced
with insight—so avant-garde.

Let it be understood
that sympathisers are fascists outside-in.
Better the pure resentments of the South
stated in black and white—enemies, friends
clearly recognisable by their skin.

Better the foul mouth,
the fist, the bomb, the placard,
than radicals turned nice,
words melting like honey
on the tongue of the blackguard

who draws the line at painful sacrifice.

2

Believing this, you overlook our common
nature, our equal rights.
When black people are likeable more or less,
I like them just the same
as more or less likeable whites,

and when they're not I don't; and I confess
that a black or a coloured woman
can stir my blood, if she's pretty,
as much as a pretty white, and if she isn't
she can't: I'm only human.

And who in a cut-throat city
should lose his living, see his family wrecked
for white men like himself, because they lack
his freedom? Yet you claim
this sacrifice for your people. I suspect

you work with an artist's passion at being black.

LET LIVE

Characters themselves, guardians of
the distinct, the precious Manifold,
they keep amid their junk
a flair for freedom, for controlled
ease. You get a stink
of garlic, a scratch of music
from an old gramophone, a wink of earrings.
Hearing them talk you know
they love their trade, its jumbled
clarities, the identities of things.

And then of people. It's a way of living
without spoiling. Here also the buyers
find peaceful outlets, resolve discords
when selfishness acquires
what shapes its opposite. (So with words,
colours and melodies loved
for being the way they are.)
Repeatedly you see faces,
especially eyes, that will respect
the beautiful or bizarre.

Unpolitical? Yes: and civilized.
Coloured folk touch the white in crammed spaces;
the traders, neither curt nor smarmy,
leave you to poke around. There are no prices
for human beings to pay but those they choose.
The only worriers are the Salvation Army,
a ladies' unit marching past in twos,
with earnest jollity banging a tambourine
('Joy Hour', it says, outside the Citadel):
gently the crowds open, gently close.

But where the road ends you meet a headline
on nuclear defence—remember then
'important commitments': big machines
that regulate little men
sold on prestige; mean ends and endless means;
warheads and racial hatred. May there be,
loitering here, a few from the tensed city
whose involvement is genuine, whose power and skill
are indispensable—renewing their innocence
by being guilty of triviality.

INTERNAL POLITICS

No—I prefer the grass,
the big trees arching,
where squirrel and owl are welcome
and the soft chirr of a mower
spurting green fountains
has joined the song of birds.

I have no faith at all
in twelve-storey blocks
and the destruction of gardens.
Ladders lead somewhere, also
fabulous beanstalks;
skyscrapers merely scrape.

Nor do I share your scorn
for art departments
and mop-haired students in the sun:
if wood could speak, those stumps
being used as chunky tables
might tell you strange riddles.

No dreamer, I abstain;
but the free poem
votes for squirrels and brimming leaves,
the artists with their odd passion,
and lots of grass
to give the machine meaning.

EARTH

She owns our native soils;
the seeds and roots are hers,
the palms, maples, firs,
the juices and the oils.

Dark ceremonies! At first
her chosen had to die
so she could satisfy
our hunger and our thirst.

Through the centuries, kings
and gods usurped her power;
image of leaf and flower
was arched by eagle wings.

Now we have learned a game
of politics and lies:
fierce jealousies disguise
how much we are the same—

one in the body's prayer
to this deep land,
with needs all understand
and permanently share,

and one because we live
by a far subtler being
than tasting, touching, seeing
catch in their finest sieve,

incomparably older
than the oldest nation,
brimming in vegetation,
in water, wind, and boulder.

No human laws determine
matter, or can make
a mountain or a lake
Italian, French, German.

THREE METAPHYSICAL SONNETS

I

Being kindred to each other, we are both
cherishers of routine. You spin the sphere
for night and day, revolve it for the year
and then the seasons, control tides and growth,
shape geometric and organic forms.
I too have many tasks, a time for each—
make my own trees and crystals out of speech,
regulate mind and body. Yet our norms
are savaged hour by hour: as forests crash
in earthquake, wind, or fire, and flowers decay
blighted or parched, my human heart is prey
to rival needs. Not chaos, but the clash
of differences, produces disarray:
your law still triumphs in the drifting ash.

II

As you exploit an atmosphere, a sea,
plasma and tissue, hand and brain, to plumb
the ocean of your Self, you'd use the sum
of all those intricacies that are me.
You ply me with incentives—fact and myth:
the first a drop of pleasure in a drought
of pain, the other shackling hope to doubt,
obsessions for the mind to sicken with.
Strange—for the very consciousness you feed
supposes I'll be garbage when you've done—
that you should risk not granting even one
reason why I should satisfy your need.
You leave me wondering what it's all about,
and yet you'd have me think and build and breed.

III

'A dreamer squatting on a pile of bones,
lost in communion. Why the sacrifice?
It isn't even he who pays the price
of his beatitude, but the unlucky dead
whose skulls the Logos used as stepping stones
to higher things.'— 'But consciousness, it's said,
is ultimately one. If that is true,
below the drops of spray called me and you
surges the ocean into which we die
from our small helpless freedom in the wind,
then come alive as neither you nor I.
Now, if you grant that some have disciplined
themselves to touch the sea and soar again ...'
—'Go on, you're doing fine! What happens then?'

TWO JAZZ SONNETS

I

I like the way they drift, not talking much,
in denim jeans and leather, with long hair
flowing across their shoulders, and an air
of dreamy patience, open to the touch
of Pan or Dionysus as they wait
for the last jazz performance to begin.
The matinée's ending now: they listen in,

hunched on the littered grass outside the gate.
Dreamy or bored? Our bodies move, but they,
the devotees, remain as still as wax.
Could be that I mythologised a sad
conformity, insensitive to the play
of drum and clarinet, trombone and sax,
with longing for the youth I never had.

II

Light fades along the river. Quiet ripples
massage the glistening mudbanks at low tide,
and car doors bang on silence. Older here,
late twenties, thirties, letting go to ease
the tensions of propriety or fear,
they stroll towards the pub in groups and couples.
The jazz-blast hits them as they step inside.
Then time gives way to tempo: by degrees
liquor and music charm divided selves
to know the strange polyphony they are.
Quick fingers fall to stillness on the keys:
that final chord ... The watcher at the bar
turns off the coloured lamps along the shelves
and bawls across the room 'Time gentlemen please'.

from **HUMOURS**

Self is your I and mine—
a something whose existence
it's practical to assume,
though deep thinkers
like Gautama and Hume
deny it. Under the influence of wine
and paradisal drugs
the self becomes a distance
valued by both contemplatives and Thugs.
Some use transcendental meditation
to melt into the Atman;
others emulate Hitler
or, if they're goodies, Batman;
survivors know their station.
My ego, I must admit,
is one of the shrinkers:
why oh why
can't it dilate a bit

when we stand I to I,
or yours seem littler.

*

Jazz: neither the grip
of perfect unity
nor the lax
unlovely scrimmage.
Trombone, clarinet, sax
like braiding water slip,
the image
of good community.

*

Magma—such stuff
as dreams are made on,
and catastrophes.
Flatulent and amorphous
yet strong enough
to open rock that lasted
centuries, it extrudes
from far below the surface.
Watch it freeze
after destruction
in obdurate attitudes
like those it blasted.

*

Cactus will stand
unmoved, unmoving, when
the water hole is dry;
spiky with acumen
will see the vultures fly,
the footprints in the sand.

*

Drill gets on people's nerves.
He knows what he's about
and never swerves.
But soon as he has gored
into the earth's quick,
and black blood gushes out,
he is ignored.
The people dance and shout—
it makes you sick.

*

Quagmire is perhaps
the nastiest of all.
To feel the blade's
temper, maybe to strike back
before the world fades,
even to fall
through space, is something;
but to lapse
in softness, to disappear
melting, melting
in the slack
lubricious hug of slime,
is dread's quintessence.
Trying to fight clear
is natural, should be told
admiringly as always; but quiescence,
turning the fear to cold
appraisal, is sublime.

*

Or: a quaking bridge
between alternatives—
the privilege
Old Nobodaddy gives,
with pedigree,
to homo sapiens.
Love makes him free,
then burdens him with chains
of choosing. What is more—
witness Adam and Eve—
the gift is spurious:
think how they had to leave,
covered in furry pelts,
for being curious—
mocked by the or
they could not use, or else.

*

Grain is the seed,
the salt,
the natural flow.
Doing the wrong deed
how shall we know,
intrinsic now, the fault

it springs from? Only pain
is certain, and the need
that goes against the grain.

*

Rowlock would like to have been
a delicate wineglass touching
a lady's lips,
or a spur
thrust in the charger's flank:
not slave between
wood and wood, crutching
a powerful lever,
envying the blade its bite,
the long shank
its swathe of air as the boat dips
and glances. You hear him grumble
quietly in his hole—
seeing himself, who might
have cut so fine a figure, in a role
unalterably humble.

*

Lustre: there were men
it haunted so, they wandered
deep in a wilderness
of forest and morass
and stinking den;
in pub and brothel squandered
their prime, and were not eased;
with searching mind
speculated, or teased
the mysteries on the page,
yet still could find
no peace; in desperation
made sacrifice, to assuage
their grief by expiation.

Some, we're told,
were never satisfied—
learned prudence, turning cold,
or till they died
raged in the fire of sin.
A lucky few
found what they'd always sought,
declared it true:
as if pure light, pure water
pouring in.

NOTES & INDEX

The following article by Richard Kell was first published in *PN Review* 106 (1995). It is reprinted here by kind permission of the editor.

The Poem and the World

Certain problems of critical theory in relation to imaginative writing have turned up again, accidentally, in *PN Review* 104. I say accidentally because, though all the contributors involved are presumably aware of those problems, only the fourth (Nicolas Tredell) draws attention to them—by mentioning the central one. The following extracts are from (1) Michael Schmidt's editorial, (2) a letter by Anne Stevenson, (3) 'A Talk with Mark Doty', (4) 'Death of a Critic' by Nicolas Tredell, and (5) 'The Beginnings of Art', a review by T.J.G. Harris.

(1) In the 1930s critical categories were politicised, with an inevitable dissipation of seriousness ... A volatile but continuous critical culture—insisting on engagement with poems—persisted through the 1960s and into the 1970s ... [The recent failure of that critical culture has to do partly with] the fragmentation of critical discourse, following on the heels of theoretical or political divisions which inevitably fragment the literature they arise from, foregrounding gender, gender preference, ethnicity, class, political complexion, requiring privileged status for the work they seek to legitimise at the expense of works of different provenance ... Is there a critic who can deal with [many different kinds of poetry, including the modern and the anti-modern], not in terms of movements or polemical positioning, but first and foremost in terms of the words combining on the page, the sounds and tones those words make, the senses they give, and how they extend or revive elements in the language we share? ... The poem will then matter once more, the main thing, the processes of making. The question will not be, 'Who made it?' but the Coleridgean, 'What has been made, how well has it been made, and was it worth making?'

(2) [Here Anne Stevenson quotes approvingly from Philip Hobsbaum's *A Theory of Communication*. The square brackets in the quotation are Stevenson's.] 'Any theory of [critical] language must be at once semantic [don't separate language from

meaning], evaluative [some works are more valuable than others], contextual [in a work of literature words should not be considered out of context] and socially oriented [criticism should relate to the social implications of the text].' ... [Now a reference to Louise M. Rosenblatt's *The Reader The Text The Poem.*] Rosenblatt ... differentiated between the paper and ink of a 'text' and the 'poem' the reader evokes or recreates ... An 'efferent' reading is a reading undertaken mainly for the purpose of gaining information: an 'aesthetic' reading implies participatory pleasure in evoking the work ... [Both Hobsbaum and Rosenblatt] worked hard to create a criticism that might show people how literary works of a high order could, as Wallace Stevens maintained, not only please people but 'help them to live their lives.'

(3) Have I done justice [in my poems] to the world I'm attempting to describe? ... Almost every poem begins with some trigger in the world—some originating image—an encounter, usually, which speaks to me in some way, which demands to be written about ... The process of writing poems was a very important part of a coming out process. I started to ask, how does all my experience ... get into the work in a way that feels responsible to [the experience]? That pushed the poems to become larger in order to hold more material, to be able to get more of the world in them.

(4) But for those who would invoke it, as much as for those who would expunge it, the aesthetic is the problem: it is notoriously difficult to define, and it constantly tends to slide into those areas which it is supposedly defined against—the psychological, the ethical, the political.

(5) It is good to be reminded, in our over-refined and theoretical age, of the realities from which the arts have grown ... [and] that the arts are not merely a bourgeois invention and the possession of a particular class, but are a fundamental part of human life anywhere ... It was, however, the biologist J.Z. Young who wrote in *Programs of the Brain* that: 'Proper study of the organisation of the brain shows that belief and creative art are essential and universal features of all human life. They are not mere peripheral luxuries. They are literally the most important of all the functional features that ensure human homeostasis.' So much for the 'uselessness' of art on which both philistine and aesthete are agreed. And as this anthology ... shows, the uses of the arts go beyond ensuring homeostasis within the individual brain, informing the whole functioning of societies and certainly not shirking the most difficult of life's realities.

Tredell's remark (4) provides the theme that underlies the following brief discussion.

Fine absolute music may help us to live our lives (2); but if it does, it does so through sounds that have no such meanings as words possess. And since the meanings of words relate to the world—language being in the first place a tool for engaging with the world—it is hard to see how, in reading a poem, we can deal with 'the senses [which the words] give' (1) without considering the world as well as 'the words combining on the page'. (I am not assuming that Schmidt would disagree.) In any case, most poems spring from a desire not only to make a word-object whose 'sounds and tones' are right, but also to say something—though at first the poet may not know precisely what—either about the real world (with or without reference to the poet himself) or about some imaginary world. It seems reasonable to suppose, then, that few poets would thank a reader for attending only aesthetically—if that were possible—to the senses of their poems' words.

Mark Doty (3) speaks of his poems becoming 'larger in order to hold more material, to be able to get more of the world in them'. This might suggest a desire above all to make poems, and to draw partly on homosexual experience for that purpose. On the other hand, Doty says 'Have I done justice to the world I'm attempting to describe?', and speaks of getting his experience 'into the work in a way that feels responsible to [the experience]', as though the poems were made not for their own sake but for a purpose which was partly social and moral. Similarly perhaps, Owen wrote 'Above all I am not concerned with Poetry. My subject is War, and the pity of War. The Poetry is in the pity.' Nevertheless we do cherish fine poems also as word-objects, some of them when the material they were concerned with has gone from the world or has ceased to be important. So it seems that the tension between a poem's existing in its own right and existing as an instrument is inescapable, burdening us with a critical problem which may have no solution.

That tension is implicit, I think, in the second and third of the Coleridgean questions 'What has been made, how well has it been made, and was it worth making?' (1). If we are to go beyond 'It was worth making because it has been very well made'—which, if true, is almost tautologously so—it seems that we can answer the third question only by turning it into 'Does this poem have psychological and then social/moral/political value?'—and hence by going outside the poem. We might also ask 'Does it have aesthetic value?'—a question indirectly concerned, like the previous one, with a listener's or reader's responses as well as with qualities of the poem. If the answer is yes, it might follow that the poem has a psychological and then a social value other than that immediately associated with its referential quality (if the latter value be allowed). At all events, the referential quality can hardly be ignored if we are to attend to the senses of the poem's words—as indeed we cannot avoid doing unless the poem is in an unfamiliar language and therefore comes across to us as nothing more than sounds and tones.

Granted that we are not to stop short at 'This poem is valuable because it is well made'—which might be to attribute artistic value without considering aesthetic value (the value of the aesthetic response to artistic quality) — how are we to deal with the poem in relation to the world it refers to or draws on? Schmidt deplores partisan evaluations—rightly if, as many of us would argue, poetry ought not to be regarded as a means of promoting attitudes, ideas, and beliefs. Nevertheless attitudes, ideas, and beliefs—from idiosyncratic to universal, with ideological or doctrinal along the way—are usually part of the referential mixture. Consequently, if our evaluations are to be non-partisan, it seems that we must try to read without prejudice a great many poems expressing or implying attitudes, ideas, and beliefs which are irreconcilable and sometimes strongly conflicting.

Can 'The Wreck of the Deutschland' and 'Song of Myself'—if we regard both as works of a high order—help us equally to live our lives (2), although the first is Christian and the second, broadly speaking, humanist? Whether or not those examples are accepted, can the same be said of numerous other poems offering divergent outlooks? My own tentative answer would be yes, on the assumption that good reading of good poetry is an act of imaginative, intellectual, and aesthetic participation. A willing suspension of disbelief is, I think, too much to ask for: a firm atheist can hardly be expected to suspend his disbelief in God while reading Herbert, or a firm Christian to suspend his disbelief in Sod while reading Larkin. But a reader might get the 'feel' of another person's experience (however inward)—as he might of Mark Doty's without having the same sexual orientation, and of Herbert's and Larkin's though his own was very unlike theirs. Given that such participation might nourish the roots of humane understanding, we could say that good readings of good poems—and, concomitantly, good poems themselves—had social and moral value.

What about poems from which the poet has disappeared— persona poems, dramatic monologues, narratives, 'philosophical' works, satires direct or dramatic? The answer could be that the poet is still present though hidden—that everything comes to us through his mind and temperament and style. (It is only for convenience that my references throughout are to men. The reading of women's work by men, and vice-versa, would be well suited to the argument.)

If good reading of good poetry is an act of imaginative, intellectual, and aesthetic participation, the imaginative and intellectual responses are to a poem's referential quality, and the aesthetic response is to its artistic quality. But the three responses are inseparable, just as the referential and artistic qualities are inseparable. If we derive aesthetic pleasure from 'Bare ruin'd choirs, where late the sweet birds sang', we do so because of Shakespeare's artistry in handling meaning as well as sound and rhythm; but we receive the meaning only by using imagination and intellect to make a connection between the poet's words and certain things we know about the world (including the effects of old age). In short, even an aesthetic response requires us to be 'outside' and 'inside' a poem at the same time. Unlike the poem's extra-aesthetic value, however, its aesthetic value is not immediately (and is only partly) associated with its referential quality: the artistic quality comes first.

Even if these suggestions were accepted, we would still be faced with the perennial paradox mentioned earlier. To say that a poem has an extra-aesthetic value immediately associated with its referential quality is to put the emphasis on instrumentality. The same is true if we say that it has aesthetic value, for this is to imply that it gives us a kind of experience which may be psychologically and then socially helpful through a homeostatic process (5). On the other hand we have a strong tendency to treasure for its own sake— not for the experiences it gives us—what is well made and perhaps beautiful. The paradox is a nuisance for critical theory, but apparently one which will just have to be lived with.

NOTES

It was hard to decide how much to give. Some readers may know A but not B, others B but not A. These pages are not for those who know both!

—*R.K.*

Firmament (p. 12)
Published in *The Bell* when I was an undergraduate. There seems to be some confusion here between the behaviour of a spiral galaxy and that of a star.

The Balance (p. 15)
See Blake's 'Proverbs of Hell' 44 and 35.

Dream and Reality (p. 43)
We're told that *meden agan*, 'nothing too much', was an important motto in Ancient Greece.

Open to the Public (p. 47)
Any historic mansion, but especially Syon House in Isleworth, Middlesex. I have taken some liberties with the statuary, but the fourth and fifth stanzas are true to guidebook information.

Metamorphoses (p. 50)
See 'The Burning Crate' (p. 10) and 'Walls: Four Variations', III (p. 76). The 'double will' near the end of stanza two is the will to good and evil, and the 'curt rubric' is a warning to bathers. The third line of stanza three alludes to Aquinas's definition *Pulchra sunt quae visa placent*, 'Those things are beautiful which please when perceived'.

Sky Poem (p. 59)
Written after a flight in a glider. The pilot told me that thermals without cloud markers are called 'blue'.

Deficient Cause (p. 64)
Augustine's idea of a deficient (as opposed to efficient) cause for the Fall—showing the influence of Neoplatonism?—can be found in *The City of God* Bk XII, chapters 6 and 7, e.g. '[The enquirer] shall find that his evil will arose not from his nature, but from his nothing.' See 'Working Late' (p. 82) and 'Famine' (p. 105).

The Dancers (p. 68)
'Logos' was for Heraclitus the cosmic principle. In Christianity, the translation 'Word' has a strong trace of that meaning when applied to divine creativity (see *John*, I, 1-5) and hence to the Second Person of the Trinity. Of course it then means also the Redeemer and the God-given scriptures. This poem is partly an attempt to recover the broader original meaning and to link it (section 5) with artistic and social creativity.—'Fret' (section 5): in NE England a word for coastal mist.
Anaxagoras, also Presocratic, used the term 'Nous' (Mind) with implications roughly similar to those of the Heraclitean 'Logos'.

Walls: Four Variations (p. 76)
Variation III, first stanza: vegetable cells and animal cells. Second
stanza: swords and courtly verse. The closing lines suggest continuity
between natural and human violence. (See 'Metamorphoses', p. 50).
Variation IV: The globes are those of pre-Copernican astronomy.

Working Late (p. 82)
See note on 'Deficient Cause'.

Friday Night (p. 92)
Recalls Hopkins' receptiveness to certain ideas of the Franciscan
theologian John Duns Scotus (1265-1308). 'Going gallant, girlgrace'
is from Hopkins' 'The Leaden Echo and the Golden Echo', and
'playing in ten thousand places' from 'As kingfishers catch fire'.

Death's Reply (p. 94)
The first line refers to familiar poems by Donne and Dylan Thomas.

To the Skylark Again (p. 94)
Written in 1970 but not included in *The Broken Circle*, this is
chronologically out of place. As a poem expressing a recurrent state
of mind it was 'reactivated' for me some years later, and I therefore
decided to include it in the fourth collection.

The Rescue Team (p. 96)
The metaphor is that of a person frozen in ice—for the poem's
psychological purposes both dead and alive.

In Praise of Warmth (p. 98)
III: Players of wind instruments like to warm them up before
performing. VII: *Wonders of Land and Sea*, a composite work I loved
to browse in at an early age, has a photograph with the caption
'When a kettle containing liquid air is placed on ice it boils, because
the ice is intensely hot compared with the very low temperature of
the liquid air'. VIII: From the same article. X: *Paradise Lost*, II, 598.
XIII: *The Revelation of St. John the Divine*, III, 16. XVI: Electric chair;
second line factual (if my source is reliable) as well as metaphorical.

The First Circle (p. 102)
Solzhenitsyn's novel.

The Butterfly Hears Tchaikovsky (p. 102)
The symphonic poem 'Francesca da Rimini' is based on Dante's
Inferno, Canto V, describing the punishment of carnal sinners.

The Slave (p. 104)
The person honoured in a Roman triumphal procession had his face
painted red. *Hominem te memento*, 'Remember you are [only] a man',
was repeated to him by a slave sharing his chariot. *Tace*, 'Shut up', is
pronounced *tahké. Me paenitet*: 'I'm sorry'.

Famine (p. 105)
'God doesn't dice': Einstein. Augustine: see note on 'Deficient Cause'. Sartre's *L'Être et le néant* (English edition *Being and Nothingness*) was published in 1943.

The Island (p. 107)
Based mainly on material from Derek Robinson's *Just Testing* (1985), including eye-witness reports.

Remembering Limerick (p. 109)
Though this has much in common with the earlier 'Holiday in Limerick' (p. 67), I regard each as a poem in its own right. My father had Irish appointments between his terms as a missionary in India.

The Victims (p. 121)
Taoist philosopher Chuang-tzu. I have drawn on A.C. Graham's scholarship. 2: Amnesty International report on Iraqi practices in Kuwait after Saddam Hussein's invasion in 1990. 3: 'He misleads or guides ... ', a recurrent motif in the Koran: see, for example, pp. 417 and 425 in Dawood's translation. 5: Sayings attributed to Jesus in the Gospel of Thomas (Gnostic).

Levels (p. 125)
Last two words: a reference to luminiferous deep-ocean fish. (See, for example, David Attenborough, *Life on Earth*, chapter 5.)

Rock and Water (p. 125)
Third stanza: two different yin-yang teachings. The second, favouring yin, is found in the *Tao Te Ching*.

Contemplative Politics (p. 127)
My reason for replacing the usual transliteration 'Tao' with Wilhelm's 'Dao' (though they are pronounced in the same way) is that the poem has reverse slant-rhymes, e.g. *jab* reverse-rhyming with *budge* instead of *badge*. But consonant couplings often change, as in *clip/pluck*. 'He-she': earthworms are hermaphrodites.

Going Forward Backwards (p. 128)
The first of eight poems with full reverse rhymes, instead of slant ones as in the previous poem.

To Lauren Newly Born (p. 129)
'Lauren' and 'Laura' (the name of Petrarch's beloved) are both based on 'laurel': L. *laurus*. Jan and Eddie are the parents.

Spring Song (p. 131)
In *The Selfish Gene*, Richard Dawkins introduced the word 'meme' to suggest the mental equivalent of a gene.

At the Summit (p. 135)
Since the fourth stanza refers to chaos theory, the last two lines may

remind some readers of patterns like the Mandelbrot set; but I've
gone out on a limb here!
The Story of Liz and Freddie (p. 136)
Black hole and orbiting star. The latter suffers the intense
gravitational pull of the former. *Event horizon*: spherical 'shell' of
black hole, within which even light is trapped by gravity. *Singularity*:
point of infinity density at centre of black hole, where the known
laws of physics break down. The theory that sucked-in energy can
reappear as a quasar 'beyond' a singularity is highly speculative.
Bardo: Buddhist term for the 'place' (non-place) between death and
rebirth. Last six lines: according to Hawking black holes can
evaporate until what's left is annihilated in an explosion of gamma
rays.—Reverse rhymes again, but sometimes anagrammatic, e.g.
sort/ astro.

Wholeness (p. 137)
Being contrary to each other, the equal spins of paired electrons are
together 'zero'. A version of the EPR (Einstein-Podolsky-Rosen)
thought experiment entailed the conclusion that, no matter how far
apart paired electrons might travel, a reversal of spin for one would
instantaneously result in a reversal for the other. Einstein, denying the
possibility of nonlocal and faster-than-light causation, maintained
that such conclusions were absurd however logical, and that the EPR
experiment therefore showed quantum theory to be incomplete. But
in 1982, having turned the thought experiment into a physical one,
Alain Aspect proved him wrong. (Einstein and his partners were
considering positions and momenta; the spin version was David
Bohm's, and Aspect, I *think*, chose photons and polarisation; but
those alternatives made no theoretical difference.) The poem's title
is explained by the fact that 'nonlocality' theory is holistic.

A Reunion (p. 142)
1: first and last lines: see beginning of *The Task* by Cowper. 3:
Donne's 'The Good Morrow' supplies 'little rooms' here and in
section 5, and 'true plain hearts' in section 1. The 'songless vaults
and raping worms' (not a quotation, of course) are in Marvell's 'To
His Coy Mistress'. 4: Dawkins' *The Selfish Gene*: see note on 'Spring
Song'. 'Pigs are machines ... ' is an inferential pseudo-quotation. 5:
A London demonstration against Thatcher's 'community charge' or
'poll tax' became violent when confronted by police.

A Spell of Churning (p. 159)
First published in 1993, but written thirty years earlier when the
poet-critic referred to was still alive. My title mimics that of his
collection *A Smell of Burning*.

Biographical Notes (p. 161)
One of my sources was the article 'Joyce and Gogarty' by Ulick
O'Connor, included in *A Bash in the Tunnel* (ed. John Ryan, 1970).

The poem was written for a collective 'Bloomsday' reading at Morden Tower in Newcastle-upon-Tyne.

Rhapsody à la Rodgers (p. 171)
Published in *Rann* (Belfast) when I was an undergraduate, this was a sincere though somewhat parodic tribute to the Ulster poet W.R. Rodgers. His *Collected Poems* were published posthumously in 1971.

Natural History (p. 173)
'Guano' is used for the droppings of bats as well as seabirds. The poem is based partly on a radio talk I heard many years before the writing.

Humours (p. 197)
'Self': Gautama's *anatta* (no-self) doctrine is of fundamental importance in Buddhism.—The Thugs (or Thuggees) of Mogul India took drugs before committing their murders.—*Atman*: Hinduism's 'universal Self'.

'Or': Blake's short poem 'To Nobodaddy' includes the phrase 'Father of jealousy'.

'Lustre': The Latin *lustrare* (from *lucere*, to shine) and *lustrum* (from *luere*, to wash) are both associated with purification: hence the last two lines of this poem. But they also have a very wide range of other meanings—sometimes surprising ones—and these are woven into the first stanza to provide something like a parable of the human spirit.

The word humours is also multi-faceted!

Title Index